NO FEAR in Love

Loving Others the Way God Loves Us

ANDY BRANER

BakerBooks

a division of Baker Publishing Group
Grand Rapids, Michigan

Published by Baker Books
a division of Baker Publishing Group
P.O. Box 6287, Grand Rapids, MI 49516-6287
www.bakerbooks.com

Printed in the United States of America

Library of Congress Cataloging-in-Publication Data is on file at the Library of Congress, Washington, DC.

ISBN 978-0-8010-1728-5

The author is represented by the literary agency of Wolgemuth & Associates, Inc.

15   16   17   18   19   20   21   7   6   5   4   3   2   1

In keeping with biblical principles of creation stewardship, Baker Publishing Group advocates the responsible use of our natural resources. As a member of the Green Press Initiative, our company uses recycled paper when possible. The text paper of this book is composed in part of post-consumer waste.

"Braner nails it with *No Fear in Love*. No simple platitudes here; just real-life stories soaked in truth that will set you free."

—**Carl Medearis**, author of *Adventures in Saying Yes: A Journey from Fear to Faith*

"Because we're both passionate about Jesus and about the Middle East, Andy Braner and I frequently cross paths. I've always resonated with Andy's spirit; after reading *No Fear in Love*, I understand why. The pathway of authentic love has led Andy past fear and into that wonderful, adventurous place where 'the other' becomes a friend. Like Andy, I'm learning that's often where Jesus does his best work in and through us."

—**Lynne Hybels**, advocate for global engagement, Willow Creek Community Church

"This is a critical and timely book that demands serious attention and reflection. Not only is our society tearing at its very fabric, but our faith has become caught up in that, and it's become a kind of 'nationalistic religious response' to the world versus a Jesus-life in the world. There isn't a subject more important yet more avoided than how we relate to others in the public square. It's amazing how we can categorize people as 'religious,' thereby invalidating the very thing Jesus told us to be: salt and light. Andy deals with this issue in a thoughtful, loving, and proactive way. He isn't merely writing ideas; he's sharing how he's lived out those ideas. When I read things like this from the emerging generation, I get really excited. Excellent read—thought provoking and challenging, with practical stories of engaging with others."

—**Bob Roberts Jr.**, author of *Bold as Love* and senior pastor of Northwood Church

Contents

Section 3 Overcoming Fear of Culture

Acknowledgments

There are so many people to thank. This book wouldn't be possible without my adventurous wife, who allows me to jet off to places where most wives would be wary. She believes in a Big God and is supportive of me and my insane ideas.

Thanks to the people at NavPress who saw this vision a few years ago, and to Baker Books for picking up where NavPress left off.

Thanks to Rebekah Guzman and her belief in my work with teens and young adults.

Thanks to the thousands of teenagers who are willing to join me on this journey of No Fear at KIVU and around the world.

Thanks to my kids Hays, Maggie, Dax, Tiki, and Gabby, who endure a dad who travels more than he should.

And finally, I'm super thankful for a God who calls us all to not fear.

Introduction

No Fear in Love

There is no fear in love. But perfect love drives out fear, because fear has to do with punishment. The one who fears is not made perfect in love.

1 John 4:18

I grew up in a fundamental, legalistic, Bible-believing family. They were wonderful and well-intentioned, and I'm thankful for the way they pursued God with all their hearts. I attended a Christian high school where teachers and coaches were committed to trying their best to give students a Christian worldview. And I ended up at a Christian college where my faith was developed even more. After my undergraduate work I even went to seminary to polish off my Christian education. I have worked for a church and for a parachurch organization, and currently I'm the president of an organization that helps teenagers to begin to understand their own faith journey in the real world.

For the last fifteen years, I've been working with high school and college students in Colorado. Our company helps students create high-adventure memories while wrestling with questions in their own faith. We ask "those" questions. Questions such as:

How do we know God is real?

Is the Bible even relevant for today?

Did Jesus really walk the earth?

Why does it all matter?

My whole life I've been taught how to be right and how to point out someone else's wrongs. I was trained to argue apologetics, to "wow" others with my worldview knowledge, and to discuss the tenets of the Christian faith so others would believe like I do. "Defend the faith at all cost!" was my battle cry. My entire educational life was spent working on what I believed to be true, and how others or "those people" thought differently than I did. I remember teachers and coaches who would use the example of counterfeit money and say things like, "You never know what's counterfeit until you study the real thing." And they held up a crisp dollar bill to somehow convince students of some metaphor of money and faith. So I studied, and studied, and even ventured into a philosophy of religion discipline where I learned how to argue with "those people" and solidify my own belief system as real, right, and true.

But when I actually met and spent time with "those people," everything changed.

I had all the knowledge that enabled me to "win" an intellectual argument, but I consistently came off like a jerk to my friends. Recently, I read the apostle Paul's admonishment to the church in Corinth and noticed the part where he says "knowledge puffs up" (1 Cor. 8:1). Nothing could have been truer in my own life. I had become the bastion of knowing *about* God but failing to know His heart in my day-to-day life as it related to others around me, especially those who didn't believe what I believed.

On my own journey to help students understand Jesus, at least in the early years, I forgot to look intently in the eyes of the One who can offer forgiveness. I was so proud of what I knew I failed to see God's heart of compassion beating loud for the world. My knowledge was puffing up. I used my intellect to demean, degrade, and judge people. And I taught others how to do the same.

I could argue the validity of Scripture. I knew how to create a system for why I believed God allowed pain in the world.

I was well-versed in evidential apologetics. I knew how to defend why I believed God was real and why the world should take notice.

I could compare any religious system to Christianity and find its obvious faults. In fact, I got so good at arguing faith I could deconstruct someone else's faith in seconds, eager to win and prideful of my own understanding.

In my personal life, I learned how to manage my own sin, punch my Christian time clock, and produce a self-righteousness only rivaled by the Pharisees of Jesus's day.

But when I tried to love others, I was just an empty gong clanging against my own intellect. I became a cold, bitter Christian only interested in converting people to Christianity, and I woke up one day wondering, *If I heard myself preaching, would I even believe in the God I speak of?*

Do I even believe this anymore?

I mean, I can make a good argument for faith, but for what?

Am I just scared to be wrong?

Over the last several years, God has used countless unusual encounters to show me how He loves others boldly, without reservation. The clear black and white lines of right and wrong that seemed so simple in my youth have blurred into a beautiful kaleidoscope to include all of the people God has created.

I no longer approach relationships with an attitude of what I can offer, but rather I have started seeing people as valuable creations, all loved by a majestic Creator.

What used to be a clear argument concerning *us* versus *them* has become more of a mystery as I've learned about the power of tradition, the lure of self-preservation, and the lust to be right. I've become well aware of my own prideful need to have the right answer, and I've started to see people through a life's lens of compassion and care.

Now when I'm asked, "How can you love _____?" my simple response is, "Well, God first loved them." Jesus even said, "By this all people will know that you are my disciples, if you have love for one another" (John 13:35 ESV).

I've come to the conclusion that we should love people not based on their performance but on the simple fact that God loves them.

It's easy to love people who look like we do, talk like we do, or even see the world in a similar way, but how many of us are willing to stretch beyond the boundaries of normal and venture into the vast world of God's creation, unsure of what we might find? How many of us are willing to invest relational capital with someone who is a Mormon or a Muslim, or who simply goes to a different church than we do?

A simple foray into the landscape of believers is a strange place. Sundays are actually some of the most segregated times in America. They're more like spiritual country clubs or rock-and-roll extravaganzas of worship with the goal of wowing others into joining the group. And I get it!

I get that every person wants to feel safe when we expose our most intimate spiritual development. I understand what it means to hide behind the safety of programs to insulate our core fears of the "other."

What if they knew who I really am?

What if they saw how I really think?

What if they try to make me believe something that's not true?

It's fear. We live in a constant need to be *something* to make sure we matter. We all want to find significance. We all want to be known. We all want to fit in one way or another.

This constant battle between our walls of protection and our true selves is what humanity is really struggling to deal with today.

Which group am I going to identify with?

Who's going to be on the right side of history?

What would God think of us if He were to return today?

We are far too concerned with the outward appearances of daily life without really addressing the core fears brewing deep inside ourselves.

What would happen if we forewent our own safety, security, and sense of normalcy for just a moment and looked into the eyes of another to connect at a deeper level?

Would we find truth?

Would we find humanness?

Would we be able to let down our barriers for even for a moment so we could experience life full of God's creation in relationship?

What would the world look like if we laid down our fear of "those people" to just begin living *with* people, not *at* them?

Would they begin to know us? Would we begin to know them?

Could we find in our collective humanity a place where common bonds are formed, and all the fear, doubt, and insecurity might fade into history?

What might the world look like if we could see people as human beings instead of objects that need to hear our intellectual arguments?

———

I've wanted to write this book for a long time. Mainly, I want to shout from the mountaintop and declare, "We need not fear people, because God made them!" I also want to create a space where our fear of others' ideas, belief systems, and religious ideologies might be put to rest in the history of peace. And I hope that we might all find a place where God's Spirit of love, care, concern, and compassion might be the core out of which we live.

I have traveled and taught people all over the world. I've been to churches and conferences from all different denominations. And you know what I've found?

Much of the Christian subculture is consumed with fear.

Fear keeps others away.

Fear creates ideological arguments.

Fear encourages the drumbeat of pride.

Fear forces us to hide in our maze of rightness.

Fear makes people run.

Fear isolates and encourages individuals to mistrust, misplace, and misuse the gifts they have in life.

We fear people living out on the street instead of in a house, so we warn our kids to steer clear of them. We fear people who speak of God in a different way than we do, so we create educational institutions to reinforce our way of thinking. We fear other religions instead of trying to engage in meaningful conversations with their adherents. We fear other cultures invading what we think is normal, so we ostracize certain groups and present a mantra of "we're right and you're wrong." We fear the sexual revolution in America today, so we attack instead of trying to learn and understand where people are coming from.

And while we create the barriers of *us* versus *them*, we find nuanced places to hide and proudly pat ourselves on the back—because, after all, we're right and they're wrong. It's almost as if we categorize people like we do sports teams. "They" wear red shirts. "We" wear blue shirts. We see the world like the Super Bowl, where the winner takes all and the loser is forgotten forever.

We protect and defend a certain way of thinking. We demand our worldview be acknowledged as right rather than engaging in the fluidity of human relationships. Anything that gets in the way of the blue shirts winning the game is considered treason.

And when fear starts to control us, we spend an inordinate amount of time trying to figure out strategies of protectionism, basically striving to act like we are normal while containing and protecting our fear deep inside us.

Think about it. At the office, a young man is afraid others are climbing the ladder faster than he is. So his relationships with the people at the office turn into illusions of friendship because "God loves all people," but deep in his heart he knows he would step over them in a heartbeat. And he may even say "God blessed me so much in my job, look how He's promoted me" all the way to the CEO's office.

At her children's school, a young mother smiles and projects her view of the world according to how she believes God has called her to act. She thinks quietly inside, *Everyone else has it together. Smile big. Everything is okay. I can do this.* But inside she struggles with feelings of inadequacy and insecurity. She sees the other moms as a threat to her own value as a mother to her kids, so she hides her struggles for fear she may be "found out."

At church, a young pastor develops new evangelism methods to meet certain people groups or designs new and exciting church programs to draw people to a particular event. He believes in his heart that if his church doesn't match the growth patterns of the church down the street, he'll be a failure. After all, God is a God of growth, not a God of stagnation. So instead of pouring into the relationships he has at his fingertips, he pushes himself and his staff to the brink of exhaustion.

It's all *fear*.

Fear we won't measure up. Fear we might be rejected by others. In the middle of fear, we think we don't matter. Or still worse, we think, *What would happen if God ever looked down from heaven and was disappointed with me?*

I find the energy and resources people spend on taming and managing fear unbelievably taxing.

What if instead we took a long look into the heart of Jesus's love for people? What if we understood the counter-cultural approach Jesus and the disciples employed to show God's ultimate plan for the earth? What if we stopped cowering in fear? We could stand up to the voices in our heads and cry, "Enough!"

There would be no more hiding in the shadows, wondering if someone else is confusing the gospel. Instead we might be able to obediently follow the One, to be confident in His love, to be sure of His compassion, and to live inside His grace. No matter the circumstance, no matter the relationship, no matter the seeming indifference, we would be encouraged to heed our call as ambassadors of the faith instead of sales-people or protectors of the gospel.

This book is a journey told through stories of my own meetings with "those people," unusual counterparts in the world who long for the same destination as I do. I believe humanity is a collection of individual people with very similar needs. We carry our experiences through life as they shape us and mold us, but much of who we are is warped inside this same awful cloud of fear.

My hope is that by reading this you will become a gentler, more caring, and more compassionate follower of Jesus. My heart's longing is to encourage my tribe of Christian brothers and sisters to take a deep look inside their own souls so that we won't be characterized by hate and fear but rather celebrated for our willingness to love others generously.

In the first section of this book I will dissect fear, share my own fear, and show how I've witnessed fear turn to triumph.

I've been blessed to meet the most incredible people who have mentored me through my fear to a place where I can see many different types of people as friends and not enemies. And in my own journey of figuring out how to love people, I've been encouraged to deal with my own "big" fears—the fear of rejection, the fear of insignificance, and the fear of failure. I hope, as I retell some of these candid stories of times when I was fearful, that you will join me by identifying people, places, or even certain events in your own life where you are most fearful. Maybe together we can overcome this paralyzing cloud.

I'm open and willing to share when I have felt afraid, and I hope you'll find the safety and security to be vulnerable and do the same as you laugh at some of my mistakes—or maybe just empathize with similar feelings. I'm not trying to elevate myself but simply to relate as best I can with people just like you who find that fear keeps us bound to the same old life, a life far from what God has outlined for us.

In the second section of this book, I'll share how I've learned to implement life lessons and knowledge into real relationships with people who don't think like I do. For a long time, I lived at arm's length from people who didn't match up with how I thought they should live—according to Scripture, of course. I want to share some significant points in my life where encounters with people of other faiths or cultures trumped my own pride in being right and helped me see people with a high need of care and compassion no matter what they believe.

Lastly, in the third section of this book, I'll share how I've been more than a little discouraged about how our culture handles current events. It seems like the media has become more about who can yell the loudest and win an argument rather than truly listening to both sides of an issue.

For me, this is all about fear. It's the fear inside that tells us, *I don't want to allow anyone to think differently than I do because that may mean I need to change the way I think,* or, *If I validate some point they have that is contrary to my own worldview, I might have to rethink my own position.* It's easy to see the fear of being wrong dictating much of the media's discussions. But if we truly want to get down to solutions to some of our culture's hottest topics, we need to stop approaching issues like a sporting event with winners and losers and start learning how to listen well to someone else's position.

This isn't easy. Listening to someone else's pain and being willing to see their position as valid can feel like giving in or condoning lifestyles and choices we don't agree with.

Humbly, I would suggest that this way of thinking is uninteresting.

Like an explorer searching for new lands, I want to understand issues on all sides and see why some people think like they do. This doesn't mean I don't have my own opinion, but it does allow me to invest my energy in truly knowing someone who is outside of my own paradigm. I'm simply trying to understand in a "stream of consciousness" way that may invite a new approach to thinking and understanding.

By no means can we figure out these issues in the pages of a book, but we can begin to forge ahead in a way of thinking that allows for relationships to be the centerpiece of arguments instead of always seeing others as potential conquests. I hope this book will raise questions that may incite further exploration into specific issues. I've found that engaging with the topics of abortion, homosexuality, and immigration in particular help raise our level of interest and bring us to a place where we can honestly ask questions about our own fear, and investigate those places where we might be able to find comfort.

Bottom line, I want us to try to develop a closer life in tandem with Jesus. I hope you'll journey with me as we learn what it looks like to love without fear.

WHAT ARE WE SO
Afraid Of?

1

The Most Fearful Time
in My Life

Do not be anxious about anything, but in every situation, by prayer and petition, with thanksgiving, present your requests to God. And the peace of God, which transcends all understanding, will guard your hearts and your minds in Christ Jesus.

Philippians 4:6–7

Sitting in the one-prop airplane, my skydiving partner looked at me and said, "What are you so afraid of?" As if this wasn't one of the most intensely fearful moments I'd ever experienced.

My wife had bought me a skydiving trip for my birthday, and somehow I found myself at 10,000 feet, getting ready to jump out of a perfectly good airplane.

What in the world am I doing here? Would they just land the plane and let me out if I cry loud enough? What if I just decide I don't want to go?

I was so scared that the blood left my face, and I sat there in the back of the plane looking more like Casper the ghost than a twenty-five-year-old adventure seeker.

The instructor, attached to my harness to guide me through this tandem experience, told me to start moving toward the door. He pushed me from behind and my fear was paralyzing. My instructor opened the door—and the noise one hears when a perfectly good door of an airplane is open at 10,000 feet is terrifying. I felt a rush of wind enter the cabin, and my body abruptly tensed as I heard the noisy whiz of the prop and sensed an incredible pressure change.

As my tandem instructor guided me into the open door, I found myself standing on the struts of the fixed-wing aircraft, and at just the right moment he yelled in my ear, "Do you want to go on one or go on three?"

And before I could answer his question, he pushed me out of the door!

Instantly, we went from the safety and security of the airplane to an all-out free fall.

Skydiving is an interesting adventure because once you're out of the plane, there's no going back. It's not like you can just say, "Hey, I'm not up for this; let's go back." Nope. Once you're out, you're out.

Falling at a crazy speed, we were flying through the air and whisking through the clouds like a bird without a care in the world. The fear I had felt in the plane was quickly replaced with an adrenaline rush I've not felt since.

"Do you want to fly this thing?" my instructor asked.

"Yeah, THAT WOULD BE GREAT!" I yelled through the loud rush of wind in my ears.

"Pull the cord!"

I obeyed. The parachute ejected from the backpack, and the rush of wind turned to serenity and peace as we slowly floated to the ground.

The instructor helped me to guide the parachute to the landing pad. "When I tell you to pull, pull down on these two handles," he said.

100 feet.

50 feet.

30 feet.

20 feet.

"Now," he commanded.

I was so full of adrenaline I yanked down hard on the two handles meant for an easy landing. For some reason our parachute took more air than either of us thought, and we started floating back upward.

"No, no, no . . ." he shouted.

And I let go.

I don't know if you've ever seen a parachute lose all the air guiding it to the ground in one instant, but when it does it loses all its fullness and flaps like a plastic bag caught in the wind.

We tumbled to the ground in a mass of parachute and humanity.

Tangled in the parachute cord, I jumped up to hug my instructor. "This is the most AWESOME feeling I've ever felt in my life!" I screamed. "Let's do it again!"

He laughed, knowing I'd just about conjured up the limit of my own courage.

From Skydiving to Love

Since my skydiving trip, I've started looking at different issues in life as if they were potential skydiving expeditions. Life is full of fearful events, and we have to take a long look into the depths of our beings to find out how much fear is really just a survival technique and how much is substantiated by a real sense of danger.

Sometimes fear can be useful. Fear keeps us safe. It warns us of impending danger.

And it drives us to certain conclusions in life.

We call it "normal," or "real life," or something "everyone else is doing," but in reality sometimes it becomes a safety net we use to feel comfortable.

From my skydiving experience, I began to wonder, *I was afraid of jumping out of the plane at first, but in reality I just experienced the biggest adventure in my life. What else am I scared of that's keeping me from experiencing life-giving adventures?*

In that moment I started to be honest about those "hot" issues in my life. I took the challenge to be vulnerable, to examine my own fear deep in my soul, and to try to identify it so instead of it controlling me, I could begin to manage it.

So What Are You Afraid Of?

Fear is such an interesting emotion.

According to a survey by the National Institute of Mental Health, the top ten human fears are:

1. Public speaking
2. Death

3. Spiders

4. Darkness

5. Heights

6. People or social situations

7. Flying

8. Confined spaces

9. Open spaces

10. Thunder and lightning[1]

Go figure. We are more scared of presenting something to a group than we are of *being dead*? On one of his *Tonight Show* monologues Jay Leno lightly joked, "I guess we'd rather be in the casket than delivering the eulogy."

Fear is a natural biological emotion we use to warn ourselves of impending danger or to shape our behavior to stay alive. It's one of the most integrated of human reactions to ensure our survival. It forces us to revert back to the safety of tribalism and connect with people who think the very same things we do. Its motivating factor is self-preservation, and it often clouds our judgment and influences our actions to the point of defining who we are.

Just think about the things you're most afraid of. Think about the things you avoid that directly affect the way you move in the rhythm of your day-to-day existence.

Are you afraid of the food you're going to eat for lunch?

Are you afraid of getting sick?

Are you afraid of wrecking your car on the drive home?

Are you afraid of the storms coming?

1. "Fear/Phobia Statistics," Statistic Brain, accessed October 31, 2014, http://www.statisticbrain.com/fear-phobia-statistics/.

Those are natural survival fears. But what about those fears that are behavioral motivators? Are you afraid of not fitting in? You may dress a certain way. Are you afraid of not making a difference in the world? You may change your vocation. Are you afraid of not being valuable? You may try to work hard to impress people so you can matter to someone else.

What are the things you fear most in your life?

Think about how many times fear commands your behavior. And then ask yourself this, inside a safe place of honesty: *How often am I willing to try to overcome my fear?*

If you're scared to speak in front of others, when was the last time you presented something publicly to a group?

If you're afraid of heights, when was the last time you climbed to a high place to challenge your fear?

When was the last time you looked a snake right between the eyes to calm your fear of reptiles? (Okay, let's not go overboard, right?)

For most of us, we would probably answer all these questions with one simple word: *never*!

We don't enjoy putting ourselves in places of risk where we fear perceived harm, potential failure, or the ever-present threat of rejection. Do we?

We just don't find those places valuable uses of our time spent here on earth. We would rather keep our lives on the paths of least resistance, keeping comfort as the core value of our existence. We don't naturally want to risk the possibility of failure, so we find ourselves in the same ruts of life, living more out of duty than out of abundance.

I'll never forget one of the most fearful times of my life as this truth stared me in the face.

The Fire That Almost Destroyed Me

It was 2002 and I was twenty-seven years old.

I was the director and manager of a $1.7 million summer ministry operation in Durango, Colorado. I hired 128 part-time employees. I hosted 260 high school students at our summer camp, now called KIVU.

I thought I was on top of the world with nothing to fear. God was moving through the ministry He had called me to. High school students were learning how to defend their faith, and the university students I hired were finding deep, meaningful relationships. It seemed like everything was going great, and the camp was gaining recognition throughout the country. We were on the verge of the next greatest ministry "thing" in America.

And then the unthinkable happened.

I was teaching a class to high school students about understanding the nature of reading the Bible. I was fed up with the way I, as a student, had been taught to use the Bible, as a "chicken soup for the soul" type of manuscript, and thought it was time somebody took the opportunity to reinvent the way students were approaching their spiritual development. After all, every youth director in the world tells their students how important reading the Bible is, and every student tries to live up to the standard of having productive quiet times in order that they might understand this Christian thing. At least they try.

In my experience, most students use the flip-and-point method. They flip through the Bible, not knowing the historical importance of how and when it was written. They have no idea how to use implications of archeology, geography, sociology, or philosophy. They've simply been told, "If you read God's Word, you'll be a good Christian." So they try to read Nehemiah, Ezekiel, or Haggai, and they have zero reference about what they're reading.

So here I was teaching students how to read the Bible in the most beautiful church on the planet. Surrounded by the giant cottonwood trees nestled on the banks of the Los Pinos River, I was living the dream. I was teaching God's Word in the most beautiful of creation backdrops.

It was a beautiful summer day. The sky was clear blue. Fifteen students were there to learn how to read their Bible. What more could a youth worker ask for?

Then, out of the corner of my eye, I saw my wife walking down the winding trail leading to our little outdoor church. She was holding a digital camera and she had a strange look on her face.

When I found a stopping place I told the kids to take a break and that I would return as soon as I found out what was going on. My wife held the digital camera in her hand and without saying a word she flipped on the playback mode of the small device. The LCD screen lit up with a picture of what looked like a mushroom cloud rising over the mountain ridge directly behind the church.

"What in the world is that?" I asked.

"We've got a problem," she said calmly. "It seems like there is a fire starting about two ridges over from us, and the firefighters say they don't have it anywhere near under control. We've got to start thinking about how to get these kids out of here."

I calmly walked back to my class, told them I had a small emergency I had to attend to, and asked that they please forgive me for cutting our class short. They were gracious, and one of the other leaders chimed in, "No problem. I'll take it from here."

I walked back to the office to see what we needed to start thinking about, but my mind was running out of control. I'd never been part of a natural disaster before and I was both scared and equally intrigued to see how this was all going to play out. I didn't have any formal forest fire training, but we had taken several precautionary measures to be prepared to evacuate if anything like this ever happened.

I called the fire department every hour on the hour for the next three days. Every time I called, I got the same answer: "It's heading north and west. There's no way that fire will ever get close to you."

But I wasn't satisfied. We polished our plans to evacuate in the event the fire started to move toward our five-hundred-acre facility. We had charts of drivers, plans for campers to flee, and a neutral spot down the valley that could shield us from any danger. The plans were in place as the fire continued to burn over the ridge, and the staff kept on going as if nothing was wrong.

Then it all changed.

One cool summer evening, I was walking out of our cafeteria and I noticed the smoke had changed directions. Instead of blowing north and west, it was now blowing straight for us. I walked up to the office, and right in front of me saw a flame jump off the top of the hill almost a half mile away, and I knew it was time to go. I raced to implement our evacuation plan, and my wife turned into the hero of the day. She orchestrated every move from that point forward to get everyone to safety as quickly as possible.

After I watched the last staff member drive out of the gates, I hopped in my own car to leave as the sheriff drove in the gates with lights and sirens blazing. "You guys need to get out of here now!" he yelled.

"We've got everyone out," I yelled back. "We're moving everyone ten miles to the south."

"Hurry! It's coming!"

We drove off, and in the rearview mirror I watched the flames of this massive forest fire rage down the mountain. It was incredible! The smell of the burning pine trees combined with the smoke-filled valley was a clear indication that everything I had worked for was about to be lost forever.

I drove down the lonely road to our evacuation spot and just cried.

I was scared.

I was alone.

I was certain this raging flame was now consuming my life's work.

For the next three weeks the National Guard set up an outpost to keep people from getting too close to the fire. They turned us around every time we tried to enter our facility, and we had to hope and pray everything was okay.

On a beautiful Sunday afternoon, the skeleton staff that remained decided to try one more time to enter our facility to assess the damage. We had already canceled our current term and were about to cancel the rest of the summer.

Again I found myself scared, not knowing who to turn to, where to find help, or how to salvage something I had spent so much time and energy working on.

When we turned the last corner, the National Guard vehicles were gone. No one was there to turn us around. No one was blocking the road.

We drove all the way up to the entrance and turned in to the camp to find that all the buildings were intact. All the landscaping was vibrantly green. All the trees were still there. The only problem we noticed was the grass hadn't been mowed in nearly three weeks.

The whole facility was untouched.

I went on an assessment walk to find out what we needed to do to get up and running quickly, only to find, well . . . everything was okay!

We sent the word out to the staff, "We're back in action; come quickly." And the university staff from all over the nation began to descend on the place they too thought had been burnt to the ground.

The local sheriff came to visit, saying things like, "I hope you know the big man upstairs was looking out for you."

The fire chief came by with a sober look and commented, "God was sure protecting this place. There's absolutely no reason these buildings should still be standing."

And it was then I knew we were called to something great.

We held a de facto worship service and began to pray. We called on the Lord to show us exactly why He had decided to spare us from the devastation felt by so many of our neighbors.

We worshiped that night like I've never worshiped before. It was one of those "Red Sea" experiences you walk through in life and wonder . . . why?

I've spent several long nights reminiscing on the different facets of that experience. So many real factors were in place, and I can't help but recall my fear during the fire.

I was so afraid. I felt so alone. I thought God had left me.

I'm embarrassed to admit my fear was paralyzing. I couldn't think straight, even though I was supposed to be the leader. I couldn't find any good in myself, even though I was supposed to be the encourager to others.

I felt like I'd lost, even though God was at work behind the scenes to save the work He wanted to continue. Even though we'd accomplished great things through the evacuation, I was holding on to this fear that I was losing everything.

If I'm honest, it was in the midst of my fear that God began to help me. He showed me that in the middle of that trial, He was there. He reminded me that amid suffering is exactly the place He always wants to work.

He helped me see my life's work isn't the most important part of who I am. Rather He is interested in growing me and helping me face the fear that often plagues my life like a cancer in my soul.

This was the real point when I decided to look at fear in a totally different way. I wasn't going to allow the fear of what I know to dictate the actions of my future. I wasn't going to allow fear of the unknown to influence my hunger for God's providence in my life. The next step: I needed to identify more places in my life where I was afraid and see how God might show up there.

2

As I Watched Fear
Take Over

Then Jesus said to his disciples: "Therefore I tell you, do not worry about your life, what you will eat; or about your body, what you will wear. For life is more than food, and the body more than clothes. Consider the ravens: They do not sow or reap, they have no storeroom or barn; yet God feeds them. And how much more valuable you are than birds! Who of you by worrying can add a single hour to your life? Since you cannot do this very little thing, why do you worry about the rest?

Luke 12:22–26

Since that forest fire, I've watched how fear works its way in my own life and in the greater culture, and I've been very interested in its effects. The years before and after my fire experience were marked by terrorism during 9/11, war in Afghanistan and Iraq, political unrest all over the world, and the widespread recession in America. It seemed like everywhere I turned there was a story to frame a narrative of fear.

I saw more and more faith groups start up those "endtimes" Bible studies in response. It seemed like everywhere I turned, Christians were more concerned with the idea that the world was coming to an end than with pointing to the beauty of a God who is interested in the restoration of brokenness. They were reacting out of total fear of what was happening around them. The center was moving, and the focus became related to the fear because, as many of my friends would ask, "How in the world can it get any worse?"

It was like we all bought into the turmoil of a world seeming to spin out of control, and gave ourselves over to the spirit of fear rather than the Spirit of love, grace, forgiveness, and reconciliation.

The bestselling books were those reminding believers of the realities of heaven and the historical demise of cultures in the past. Many of my friends turned into survivalists, storing away ammunition and food as they faced the impending "end of the world."

The number of handgun permits skyrocketed as people were grasping at something they could count on if the world really took a nosedive and they had to protect their families. People stocked up on food to eat if their communities were destroyed by some terrorist attack. I saw the price of gold hit $1,800 an ounce as even investors were looking for safeguards from the Wild West of Wall Street. (Even my own grandmother was packing a 9mm just in case!)

The world bought into fear, and fear was clouding the line between what was really going on and what might be going on. It was almost like fear was controlling the news, the church, and the communities where people lived. It caused so many people to act out of their natural tendencies and resort to new ideas as everywhere they looked the sky was falling.

You might think people who believe in God would be immune to this type of behavior, but I found it to be quite the contrary. People of faith, those same people who believed God was in control of all things, were allowing fear to change the message of the gospel instead of reaching out and helping solve problems. I found myself in conversations about how sin was "changing everything in our known world." Christians wanted to talk in condescending tones about things like the homosexual movement, the abortion debate, diminishing religious liberty, a new church opening down the road that threatened to take away the members of their own faith community, and the man on the side of the street who didn't smell or look right or live in a world that seemed successful to onlookers.

All in all, I was sensing an air of contempt. It was almost like everyone needed to find something we could point out to make our lives seem a little more, well . . . sane. We were all allowing the events around the world to create a cloud of fear, dictating the conversations in our own backyards. Fear was beginning to grip our thinking, hope was fading in the distance, and we needed something, anything, to bring us back to what was deemed normal before.

When the tentacles of fear begin to sink into our psyche, we begin producing symptoms of a protective attitude. We look around our world at everything we have accumulated and we start feeling the uncomfortable fear of change creeping in, *and that's scary*!

We have to protect the status quo. We have to protect civilization and our traditions as we know them. We have to protect our own version of the worldview we hold as true.

And many of my Christian friends started with a protectionism as a foundation of their faith. They were determined to protect the gospel.

Protect the Gospel?

I must admit, I find people in faith circles who fear extremely interesting. History gives us a primer on how the church has tried to protect the gospel at the expense of human life. Whether it was Copernicus, Galileo, or even Martin Luther, we have a long line of black eyes when protecting the gospel became more important than loving people. Church history is full of people being burned at the stake, boiled in oil, or crucified for thinking outside the normal realm of cultural fear and trying to bring hope.

Although we might not resort to those extreme actions, people interested in protecting the gospel today often are people who don't have a realistic way of seeing and knowing the gospel. What does it even mean *to protect the gospel*? Do we really think there's an inherent duty for Christians to be the bastions of faith in the face of anything the world might throw at us? Maybe what the uncertainty of events shaping our world really causes us to protect is our version of the gospel or the tradition we think of as the gospel.

"Stand up for your faith" is a mantra I often deal with when I speak to various churches around the world. But do we really have some kind of play when it comes to the structural integrity of what God is doing on earth? A cursory description of God would be that He indeed is the Creator of all things, the Firstborn over all creation, the Beginning and the End, and in Him all things hold together (see Col. 1:15–20).

So when I meet someone who is fearful and finds the need to "protect the gospel," I wonder, *What God do you actually serve?* If God is a God who sits on the throne of heaven and earth, what do you have to be afraid of? Honestly, what in the world can you fear once you see God as the Master of the universe?

We can watch financial institutions collapse and know that God is in control. We can stand up for right, and even if we lose we know God is in control.

We can watch our culture take in a deep breath of depravity, and we can rest in the fact that God is still on the throne of heaven and earth, and in Him all things hold together.

Jesus spoke of fear more than once, and in Matthew 10:28–31 He encourages the disciples:

> Do not be afraid of those who kill the body but cannot kill the soul. Rather, be afraid of the One who can destroy both soul and body in hell. Are not two sparrows sold for a penny? Yet not one of them will fall to the ground outside your Father's care. And even the very hairs of your head are all numbered. So don't be afraid; you are worth more than many sparrows.

Do we really believe that?

Do we believe that we are worth more than the sparrows God created, which He doesn't allow to fall to the ground without His knowledge?

The Fear of Not Being Worthy Enough

In 1998 I was in the delivery room at a hospital in Springfield, Missouri. My wife had just endured about fourteen hours of labor to deliver our firstborn son, Hays.

The doctor came back in the room after doing all the stuff they do to newborn babies and handed me this little baby wrapped in what looked like a dishrag. "Here you go. Meet your new son."

All of a sudden this unbelievable feeling of fatherhood swept over me. *I can't do this! I'm only twenty-two years old. What business do I have being a father?* I started imagining all those things dads are supposed to teach their sons. Would I be good at teaching him how to throw a baseball? Would I remember to teach him how to change a tire? What if I forgot to help him understand how to make good friends? Or what if I totally botched the "birds and the bees" talk?

I almost felt like I needed to hand him back to the doctor and say, "Hey pal, you've got a degree in this stuff; maybe you ought to take this one. I'm not sure I'm ready."

I sat in that hospital room feeling totally unworthy, but at the same time this pride and protectiveness washed over me. My wife, Jamie Jo, had left for a moment, and there we were in the dim light of the hospital room, just me and this little guy.

Sometimes in life we feel as if God is so distant that we have to be the protectors. While we see the world spinning out of control, we look up in the night sky and since we can't see God, touch God, smell God, or audibly hear His voice, we have this sense we need to wrangle our own spiritual arms around Him and protect the message He gave us. We become the new father welling up with emotion. We can't believe He's given us such grace. We don't know how in the world we can keep that sensation pure. But with all our effort, with every fiber in our being, we feel as though we are the protector of the gospel and nothing will get in the way of the safety and security of this message.

And in an instant the tables turn. We recognize we have been given the most delicate of existences. Our bodies are frail. Our minds can't comprehend a lot of what God tries to help us with. And we can give ourselves over to the fear of being unworthy. We become like that baby wrapped in the dishrag, helpless to know what to do without a Father who will protect us.

Jesus's message to the disciples in Matthew 10 was revolutionary. He was sending them out for the first time to tell people of the kingdom of heaven, and it must have been quite a shock. Remember, He told them they were about to be rejected, be flogged in the synagogues, and probably endure much persecution. Then He gave them the best locker room encouragement speech ever told.

Don't be afraid. Don't worry; I'm with you. Don't get discouraged; I know the number of hairs on your head. Believe me, you're worth more than even the smallest of birds on the planet.

I love you.

And still, they must have walked with a fear-filled sense of reality as their world was about to spin out of control.

Don't we do that?

We try to make faith the foundation layer of our entire lives, and yet still we sense this frail unworthiness. We're afraid that things won't turn out like God has already told us they will. We fear we may fail God somewhere. And if we're really honest with ourselves, we fear we may not actually believe what He told us.

We have a serious fear problem, and much of it centers on our own understanding and belief in the One True God. It doesn't mean there won't be moments in life when you have to face your fears, but to couch the fear as a battle cry to protect the gospel elicits a realistic question: What kind of God needs our protection?

Whether we're staring in the face of a massive forest fire or we're looking into the darkness of depression, fear can have an unrelenting hold on our emotions. It has the ability to take our eyes off of possibility and instead focus our emotions on the worst-case scenario. But the most discouraging part of fear I have found is this: we like it.

The Fear of Actually Succeeding

Our culture is addicted to fear. We like movies that cause us to cover our eyes and sink down in our chair. We love the news media that promotes fear as a part of their agenda.

Fear sells in our culture. And Christians have bought in—hook, line, and sinker. We are far more worried about watching the world around us sinking into the muck and mire of war, godlessness, and immorality than we are about actually watching for God to succeed. We don't really believe it will all turn out okay because we spend a major part of our lives worrying.

What if I die?

What if I lose my job?

What if my friends leave me?

What if I don't measure up?

And somehow when we start to gain traction in any of these areas, we feel like something's not right, and we run to the things that cause us to fear. Like a hamster on the wheel of life, we keep going round and round, never taking an opportunity to hop off.

As I was observing this "run for the hills" cultural phenomenon, I began to wonder: What if fear is actually keeping us from experiencing the fullness of life Jesus came to provide? What if fear is actually acting like a container, keeping us satisfied in our own corner of comfort?

In John 10:10, Jesus says, "The thief comes only to steal and kill and destroy; I have come that they may have life, and have it to the full." Why do we always focus on the thief instead of taking ample time to focus on the full life? What if we started to see the world through a lens of abundance rather than remaining paralyzed by the things we're most afraid of? What would that look like?

1. We would be able to share our lives with people who need us.

I work with teenagers and college students, and if you want to see fear in its purest form, just take a stroll through the hallways of today's high schools to see insecurity at its fullest. Every student I've ever met has a predetermined idea of what it means to be popular or successful, and they spend an inordinate amount of time trying to put on a show to protect their deepest insecurities from their classmates.

Not that long ago, I was speaking at a retreat for a Christian school. I was intentionally trying to develop a fertile ground of conversation where students would feel comfortable facing their fears. I have to say, it's not easy to look a student in the eye and open a line of communication with unabashed trust, but it's my goal to make sure students understand I'm in the same boat they are. There's nobody on the planet who can claim a spotless life free from the baggage we all carry. So when students see the vulnerability in my own heart, they welcome me to the place where they can explore the fear they experience.

On a cool evening after my final session, one of the football players decided he was ready to talk to me about his embarrassing fear. This guy was well respected by his peers. He could be the poster child for the school. We sat outside the auditorium and he started. "I'm addicted to . . ." and his voice faded off.

"I'm sorry, I didn't catch that."

"It's just, I feel so embarrassed. If anyone knew what I'm about to tell you, I would risk *everything* at this school."

"It's okay. I've got this. You're not going to tell me anything I haven't heard in my fifteen years of youth ministry." I tried to calm him.

"It's just . . . I'm addicted . . . I'm addicted to watching men online gain weight," he confessed.

"I'm not sure I'm following you. What?"

"There are videos online called 'gainers' where men take before and after pictures of themselves gaining weight."

I was wrong. I'd never heard this one before.

"When I watch these videos I'm attracted to the men in them, and I just don't know what to do. I know it's so wrong. Can you help me?"

Now, in any normal counseling session, a trained professional might be able to keep a poker face, but I have to admit I was shocked. I'd never heard of this before, and I had a decision to make. Either I could look the young man in the face and make sure he understood how wrong this was, or I had an opportunity to empathize with his *real* pain of embarrassment, fear, and addiction. I could begin by living life "with him" instead of conjuring up all the reasons he was wrong and thereby living life "at him."

If we take a position in the world where we have to live on a mountaintop of purity without being able to sit with people who are hurting and in real fear of what they're doing, we can allow fear to make us run. I decided it was time to engage, and over the course of the next hour I tried to understand where this desire came from, why it was such an addictive behavior, and what I could do to pray for my newfound friend. Ultimately, we had to find a special counselor for him, and today he's doing really well. He is married, has two kids, and has a great job. The fear that allowed the thief to take over has faded into his distant past.

There are several youth programs around the world that coach students to be sure they hang out with the "right" people. The leaders are intent on making sure they have a clean, pure group. I've even found adult groups so intent on making sure they are avoiding sin *and people dealing with sin* that they don't have a place where people can go to confess the areas of their lives in which they are struggling. We've created spiritual country clubs instead of spiritual hospitals. Understanding how to put God's provision before thoughts of self-preservation allows us to engage with people who really need help.

2. We wouldn't hide our faith.

In 2012 I was working with an American group settled in Saudi Arabia. It's always been my practice to respect the groups who invite me to their homes when I'm traveling, and this was no exception. Usually I like to know what's going on in the group and how I can bring a message of hope to a particular situation. It's not my style to just go to a place, conjure up some canned message I learned, and recite my best sermon. So we spent a few conference calls talking about how I could be best used while I was there.

During one of these conversations, one of the event organizers said to me, "Okay, I think this will all work out great. But while you're not speaking is there something you'd like to see while you're here? After all, it's not every day you have access to some of the most interesting sites in the Middle East."

I thought for a second, and just before I spoke another organizer piped up. "Maybe you want to go and see an oil rig?"

An oil rig? I thought.

"No offense to you guys or the work you do, but I can't think of anything more boring than hanging out on an oil rig," I tried to tell them diplomatically.

"Well, what would you like to do?" he asked.

"I want to go meet with an imam and talk about our differences of faith."

And silence was on the other end of the phone.

"Sorry, did you guys lose me?" I asked, wondering if the connection was sketchy.

"No. No. We're just wondering how we can pull something like that off. You see, we've lived over here for nearly fifteen years, and we've never had dinner with a Saudi family. It's just not something we do," he replied.

I was shocked.

I wondered why people would live in a world where they could make friends with people of a different culture, a different religion, and a totally different way of life, and not take that opportunity. In this one short conversation, I found my purpose.

When I arrived in the small American compound I began a week of encouraging my fellow believers. One night, I made some kind of statement like, "The two most important things a faith journeyman can do is to love God and love others. If you're missing either of these two points, you're missing out on the abundant life God gave you."

After the meeting was over, a man walked up to the front and asked, "So you want to meet real Saudis?"

"Of course I do," I answered.

"I'm coming to pick you up at your hotel at 9:30 tonight. I want to take you to a place that might stretch your principles."

I wasn't sure exactly what he meant, but I try to live my life with a constant *yes* in mind. I kind of have a reckless view of life that draws me to adventure. So traveling through the Saudi Arabian countryside to meet people who think differently than I do was a real thrill.

At 9:30 p.m., my new friend pulled his car up to the front of the building. I got in, pulled my seat belt over my lap, and asked, "So, where are we going?"

"I have a friend who owns a luxury room at a hookah bar outside of town. I told him about you and he wants to meet you."

All of a sudden I had a choice to make. I'm not sure what my evangelical friends would think of me frequenting a Saudi hookah bar, but something in my soul whispered, *Just don't be afraid.*

We traveled a few miles out of town to a dark warehouse district dusty with the new sand that had been brought in from the afternoon sandstorm. I looked around feeling intimidated by the environment, wondering if this was going to be the end of my short ministry, maybe even the end of my short life. I've seen the videos of Middle Eastern men clashing with westerners, and there was a tense atmosphere around the world between Muslims and Christians that caused the hackles on the back of my neck to rise like a radar warning of danger.

"It's okay, you're going to love this." My new friend tried to calm me down.

We pulled around the last corner to the front of a building bright with neon lights. Cars lined the roads, the sheer number of people there that night emphasizing the popularity of this nightspot. My friend called on his cell phone, speaking Arabic to our host, and then said to me, "Okay, we're set."

We exited the car, walked into the neon building, and proceeded to the elevator. We traveled to the fourth floor and walked through another long hallway to a door with one of those secret windows at the top. My friend knocked, the window slid open, and then the door opened to reveal about fifteen Saudi men all reclining on the floor, with hookah pipes all over the room.

I must admit, fear began pulsing through my veins.

To date, all I knew about Muslim men in groups is they weren't fond of Christians. America didn't exactly have the greatest reputation at the time, and all I could think was, *I have two strikes against me. American plus Christian equals what?*

Our host greeted us with a smile and offered us a large platter of hot Saudi food. He asked me to sit near him and I sheepishly walked over to sit beside him. My new friend stood in the middle of the room and announced, "Gentlemen, this is Andy. He's from America, and he's not with the CIA," which was approved with belly laughs from my new Saudi friends.

For the next half hour I sat and listened to this man talk about his family, his business, and the time he spent with his buddies in the remote hookah bar.

"So how do you guys do the whole four wives thing?" I asked inquisitively. (Muslim men have the option of taking up to four wives in the kingdom.) My new friend laughed and just waved off my question as an American who didn't know how Saudi culture worked.

"Are you a Christian?" he asked pointedly.

All of a sudden the fear of being in the middle of the Saudi desert with people I didn't know began to weigh heavy on my mind. My pulse started speeding up, and I didn't know what to do. *If I answer this one wrong, I might be on a YouTube video begging for my life*, I thought. But with the Spirit guiding me, I answered the question I was asked. "I don't know exactly what kind of Christian you're referring to, but I do follow Jesus of Nazareth," I said.

"Oh good! I've been looking for someone I can talk with about the life and nature of Jesus. Would you tell me what you know about him?"

And in that moment, everything changed.

My fear subsided. My pulse slowed down. I didn't fear for my life. In fact, I felt as though I was in the midst of friends, not enemies.

Our conversation was rich with culture, religion, and respect. For the next two hours we discussed the life and times of Jesus in the Bible as related to the message from the Quran. It was amazing!

I had been so afraid of the stereotypes—my fear compounded by the constant affirmation from the media, my friends, and my mentors—that I forgot one simple lesson. Jesus said, "And surely I am with you always, to the very end of the age" (Matt. 28:20).

I don't need to be afraid. If I live my life through the paradigm of Jesus and make friends who are attracted to that life, then I don't have to fear they'll reject me because I tell them my story. I've actually found the opposite is true most of the time. When I explain why I live my life the way I do, they're often more intrigued and continue to ask questions. Remember, people are people, and most people are interested in learning about others.

3. We could engage in a world where people are seeking a place to belong.

I'm not sure if you feel this way, but if I'm honest with myself, the fear someone will see me for who I am and walk away, rejecting me, pings on the deepest part of my soul. I know I'm not alone in this journey. I work with high school and college students. I work with faith groups. I work in a world that defines people by categorical compartments.

And I've found that the same fear of rejection I help counsel my students through is primed and ready for me to experience too.

A few years ago, I had a unique invitation to accompany a group of American Christians to the Middle East. I was just beginning my exploration of world religions through the lens of leadership and development for high school and college students, and I could not have been more excited. Our first stop: Beirut!

At the beginning of our trip, I decided to take a different airline than the rest of the group. The truth is, I had accumulated a few more reward miles, and it was going to be a huge cost savings if I traveled separately. So I set out to Beirut all by myself, ready to meet our group when they arrived.

To work out the logistics, I called the team leader and told him, "I'll just wait in the Beirut airport for a few hours until you guys get here, and then we can go together to meet our hosts."

"No, really," he said. "You don't want to wait in the Beirut airport. There's nothing to do. Just grab a taxi out in front of the airport and give them the address to our host home. They'll get you all set up, and then we'll arrive about six hours later," he instructed.

"Wait, what?" I tried to hide my surprise. "You know, I've never been to Beirut. I don't know these people. Isn't this the city known for violence and extremism?" I was feeling that sense of rejection creep inside my soul, and I wanted to protect myself from any hint of that feeling. "Seriously, I'll just wait." I tried to convince him this was the best idea, the tenor in my voice revealing the fear bubbling up inside me.

"Braner, you've been around the world. Don't worry. They know you're coming early, and everything will work out." He knew exactly what I was trying to get out of, and to this day I think he was trying to mentor me through my own feeling of rejection.

"Okay, I guess I can try. But what happens if . . ." I started to trail off.

"Just get a cab. See you there." And he hung up the phone. He was obviously finished with my reasons for why this wasn't going to work.

So one flight later, I found myself in an Arabic country known for its violent past, without any idea of where I was going other than a text I received from our team leader that led to an apartment building where I was going to meet the hosts I'd never met.

How in the world did I get myself into this one? I thought.

The cab ride was uneventful—that is, if you consider a cab driver who drove at breakneck speeds through an unknown city as ordinary. He didn't speak English. I didn't speak Arabic. So I sat in silence with whispers of confirmation of my own safety swirling about. *This is such a bad idea.* It would be a miracle if I even made it to the address in the text message.

We arrived at the building about an hour away from the airport, and I grabbed my luggage. Walking up to the doorman, I was totally scared to be left out in the cold. Here I found myself in an unfamiliar city, standing next to a building I had never seen, ready to meet people I'd never seen, who were supposed to take me in. This was crazy!

I worked my way past the doorman and found the elevators. I pushed the button to the top floor. *Braner, this is so stupid*, I kept telling myself. *God, if you get me out of this one . . .* And I proceeded to make as many deals with God as I could think of. Ever pull that card?

As the elevator slowly made its way to the penthouse, I just prayed, *God, I know I'm here for a reason. Please let this one work out.*

I knocked on the door to the apartment and was greeted by one of the most hospitable hosts I've ever known. Through broken English he said, "We've been expecting you, come on in."

As I walked into the lavish penthouse suite, I noticed several Arabs in the living room engaged in what seemed like an incredible conversation. "Okay, now we only speak in English," my host boldly informed the other guests.

I was amazed. I didn't even know this guy, and he was willing to change the whole course of conversation to accommodate my understanding. My heart was won right there.

They had assembled an evening dinner party with their friends to begin the multifaith discussions. Evidently, they were expecting the group to arrive sooner than was possible, so instead of having ten American Christians to talk to, a neighbor, a pastor, an imam, and several friends excited to talk about faith ended up with . . . well . . . *me*.

My luggage was taken to the guest room, and my hosts invited me to sit and discuss world events in light of the great religious divide.

We talked about the nature of Christian thinking in America. We talked about the fear of Islam and extremism. We worked through the Great Commission, the Great Commandment, and the similarities and differences inside of the Christianity/Islam debate. It was absolutely fascinating.

I must have lost all track of time because no sooner had I chased this religious dialogue into the black hole of conversation than I heard a knock at the door. It was the other members of our team, arriving late. Our host gave them the same hospitable welcome, and right there in front of everyone I heard him say, "I'm excited for our time together for the next few days. I rarely meet Christians like your friend Andy."

Suddenly all those fears of being in a new city with a different people group faded away. I felt like I was accepted into the group and was valued as a participating member in some real work that might pave the way for many to begin living like Jesus.

It was as if I had walked into this vast cloud of the unknown, holding desperately to my belief that God had all things under control, and now I was being introduced to some of the most influential people in Lebanon. I'd made it, and I didn't have to be scared anymore.

As I look back on my time in Beirut, I find a growing confidence emerging. I start asking questions. Why was I so afraid? Who was I afraid of? Why did I feel so uncomfortable going on this trip when we were going to talk about Jesus anyway?

Doesn't God say I'm more valuable than the sparrow? Didn't Jesus confirm to the disciples that God has the hairs on our heads numbered? Why do I want to give in to fear instead of giving over to the still, quiet confidence provided by knowing there is a greater Power willing to take care of me?

And then I begin to think about all the people I interact with who hold the same fears. What would we do if we had an opportunity to make a global impact in the midst of influential leaders? Would we be scared? Would we be anxious? Would we rise to the occasion and be the ambassadors of faith we are called to be?

I wonder, where does this fear come from? Am I crazy to think there is a place where we can just exist together as humans, even if we believe in different ways of living life?

Through my Beirut trip, I found a well of confidence to allow God to be who He is in my life. I don't have to be afraid of rejection. I don't have to feel that sense of unworthiness. And I certainly don't have to give in to the fear of failure.

Who I am isn't about what I look like or how good an argument I can put together. I can stand in the presence of people who think differently than I do, no matter what their position of authority and influence, and be the man God made me to be. That's the same God who created all we see, holds all things together, and desires nothing greater than the world coming back into rightness with Him.

What's so crazy is that most people in the world long for this sense of security and still lack the necessary confidence it takes to stand in the presence of their fear and command it to obey them instead of the other way around.

Life is a constant battle wrestling with the fear we hold inside. I don't have this one all figured out, but every time I allow life's experiences to play out, I get another small grain of confidence. Fear takes a backseat, and I realize I don't have to protect the gospel; it's actually protecting me.

3

A Fearless Heart
of Understanding

Blessed are those who fear the Lord, who find great delight
in his commands.

Psalm 112:1

The Christian community has a strange vibe to it when you look from the outside in. Believe me, I get it. I grew up in a Christian home, went to a Christian school, and then to a predominantly Christian university. I went to a Christian seminary, and for the first fifteen years of my professional life I worked for Christian organizations. I can make a good case that I am a true professional Christian.

I've used the strange language often used by my tribe. Words like *accountability*, *authentic*, and *relevant* often shape our talk, but when used outside the confines of the Christian culture this lingo brings a sense of confusion in understanding what we really mean. Phrases like "guard my heart," "keep my eyes pure," "have my quiet time," "walk the Romans road," and my all-time favorite, "give it up and give it to God," may be normal to people who think like us, but to the real world it's just gibberish. I like to call it *Christianese*.

When you're on the inside, these phrases make sense. Anyone who grew up in church knows what this stuff means. We all do this, and it's not that strange to me when I hear it in the right context. We all apply the historical church baggage we carry to every situation and just roll with the phrases we picked up along our Christian journey. But what if you're someone who didn't grow up inside Christian circles?

Have you ever heard someone start a prayer by saying something like, "Dear Lord, thank You for bestowing all Your grace upon us"? How many times have you ever heard anyone really talk like that in real life? Why do we do this? Have we learned to pray certain words just because we've always prayed that way? What do our friends think of us when we use that language? Or better yet, what do new people who are searching for meaning through faith think when we cloak our phrases with some sort of semantic symbolism only afforded to the most astute Christian students? Where are the places that people can be understood in our community?

It wasn't that different in Jesus's day. Luke 9 tells a story of Jesus that I have learned from in my search to understand fear and resentment. It goes like this:

> As the time approached for him to be taken up to heaven, Jesus resolutely set out for Jerusalem. And he sent messengers on ahead, who went into a Samaritan village to get things

ready for him; but the people there did not welcome him, because he was heading for Jerusalem. When the disciples James and John saw this, they asked, "Lord, do you want us to call fire down from heaven to destroy them?" But Jesus turned and rebuked them. Then he and his disciples went to another village. (vv. 51–56)

It seems like such a strange story in the middle of the Gospel of Luke, but it carries great significance.

The disciples didn't have a forest fire threatening to burn their ministry to the ground, but the roadblocks to accomplishing what Jesus asked them to do were in place. After all, Jesus was heading for His final days in the town of Jerusalem, and the disciples who were traveling with Him were responsible for making the necessary preparations. They were in charge of things like where they would eat, where they would stay, and how they would travel. In our churches today we may assign those tasks to the "organizational committee."

So you can imagine the sense of failure they felt when someone actually stood in the way, refusing their planning sessions.

These disciples walked with God. They talked with God. They saw Jesus performing miracles. They knew a good work was at hand. And in the midst of that good work, a band of Samaritans stood in the way.

I wonder if they were angry, scared, embarrassed, or just afraid of what Jesus might say when they returned empty-handed. The disciples were on a mission, a mission greater than any ministry the world had ever known. There was a significant importance to what they were doing, and they knew Jesus had the power to clear the way through these crazy people.

When the word got out the Samaritans weren't going to allow Jesus to come through their town, there were some interesting responses from the disciples that might outline some of the same components of fear we still feel today.

The Religious Culture

This wasn't simply a refusal of service. There are enough history books to fill libraries all about the way the Jews and the Samaritans interacted. A Jewish man would never set foot in the company of a Samaritan, primarily because of their heresy. The Samaritans were people who thought God existed in the temple they erected instead of the temple in Jerusalem where the Jews worshiped. The Jews saw the Samaritan culture as one that committed ultimate blasphemy toward God.

You can imagine there was a less-than-polite disconnect between the two cultures, and their hatred for one another was distinct and palpable throughout the New Testament.

Have you ever known two groups like these to meet at a table of religious discourse? What about the constant feuds between churches today over who actually cornered the market on truth?

When I was learning the principles of the church, I can remember my Protestant Sunday school teacher trying to convince me the Catholic church was against God. He told me they prayed wrong. He told me they worshiped idols. He told me the pope was the antichrist coming at the end of the Bible in the book of Revelation. This animosity toward the "other" in my own community was probably similar to the animosity the Jews felt toward the Samaritans of Jesus's day.

But when you boil all the disagreements down to the bottom line, we're just afraid. Catholics are afraid Protestants are living outside of God's will. Protestants are afraid Catholics worship idols.

Both groups have to create a reason for being different than the other, and their core fear has brewed hatred, violence, and a history of Jesus-followers who are more concerned with their need to be right than they are for people.

The Racial Culture

We can't overstate the fact that when Jews were around Samaritans there was a dramatic effect on their interpersonal relationships. They didn't have anything to do with one another for fear of becoming social outcasts. The Samaritan heritage was mainly a genetic effect. When the Assyrian army conquered the Jewish nation, Assyrian men took Jewish women as their wives. Their offspring were called Samaritans, and they were seen as outcasts inside the "pure" Jewish genealogical structure.

If a Jew was seen with a Samaritan, other Jews might think he wasn't loyal to his family heritage. If a Samaritan was seen with a Jew, his countrymen might brand him a traitor. There were significant racial conflicts shrouding the Jews and Samaritans during Jesus's time. Racism was a part of Jesus's day. And racism clearly plays a part in the tense attitudes we have toward others. The fear of the "other" and misinformation about certain people groups cause us to erect walls of protection.

We're afraid if someone doesn't look like us or lives in a different region than we do. It's natural for our psyche to immediately try to categorize them as someone who may pose danger to our way of living. It's part of protectionism. Even in America, in the biggest melting pot of ethnic diversity ever known, the bigotry accompanied by racism is alive and well even today.

In 2007, my wife and I decided we wanted to adopt internationally. We already had three biological children, but the urge to be a part of God's calling on our lives was palpable. James 1:27 says, "Religion that God our Father accepts as pure and faultless is this: to look after orphans and widows in their distress and to keep oneself from being polluted by the world."

After reading through James, I asked my wife, "Do we know any widows? Or do we even know any orphans to take care of?"

It was pretty clear at the time that our religion had been reduced to attending church, committing to local Bible studies, and talking that *Christianese* everyone in our community was using. But we really weren't doing anything of significance to live a life of pure and undefiled religion.

After receiving a call from a friend of ours in Rwanda who ran an orphanage, we decided to adopt the last little baby dropped off in front of their facility. I knew this was going to be a good thing, but in the back of my mind I also knew our Christmas pictures were going to look a little different from this point forward. At the time we had three white American suburbanite kids, and now we were going to welcome a black African girl to live in our home. I wasn't sure how my friends or family would respond, but I knew things were going to be different.

When little Gabby came home, we were elated. Our home was loud with the sounds of a baby, and we were so excited to begin this journey of raising a multiracial family. One thing I didn't consider was that at the time we lived in a pretty small southern town with a long history of white and black racial tension. And the journey got a lot more interesting.

When my wife went to the local supermarket, people would ask, "So, where did you get her?" as if Gabby had been part of a pile of cantaloupes we had rummaged through. Or they would say, "Oh, where is she from?" as if we somehow just traveled someplace on a mission trip and impulsively picked up a poor little black girl as a souvenir.

The African Americans in our community, who were few at the time, looked at us like we were trying to assuage some "great white flight" guilt for a little African girl, and we got snarling looks from afar. I had no idea in 2007 that people still saw the world through this lens of "us versus them," but when my little girl became the object of this ignorant talk I wondered how much more was going on behind the scenes that I had never seen.

Here we were trying to follow one of the most important commandments in the Bible, and even my fellow Christians were creating these funny walls of "us versus them."

Don't be deceived, racism is alive and well in our world today. Don't try to convince yourself any differently. I've seen it firsthand.

Racism is the culmination of ignorance and self-preservation. We all have bias, however unintentionally, against people who look different than we do. We see someone who looks different and a flood of historical bias sweeps through our being, and all the stereotypes we know come to the surface.

The interesting part of racism is that when you take a risk to get to know someone who looks different than you, usually you'll find a fellow human who is also dealing with the same bias. Fear is what causes people to be unwilling to take that risk to really know and be known by someone else. Jesus helped us see this play out in the story of the Good Samaritan, but we'll get to that in a bit.

The Reconciliation Refusal

As you can imagine, with racial issues added to the religious conflict between Jews and Samaritans, there weren't many meals shared between the two groups of people.

They weren't seen in public together. Their kids didn't play with one another. Businesses were kept separate, and reconciliation was far from the minds of the people. The fear of risking their own identity and reputation kept them from any social association. It was as if there was never any room for reconciliation, and generation after generation was taught how to hate.

And it really isn't that different in our world today, is it?

Take an inventory the next time you sit down in the church you attend.

Sure there are progressive churches calling on communities to engage in multiethnic worship today, and some are overcoming this notion of "my tribe versus your tribe." But most of us go to worship in places where people look like us, make about as much money as we do, live in similar cultural communities as we live, and believe the exact same things as we do.

A friend of mine once told me, "Today, the most segregated time in the American week is on Sunday morning." And you know what? He's right.

I think the story of the Jews, Samaritans, and disciples is quite interesting as two very different characters must engage with one another in primary relationships.

The Jewish disciples ask for help.

The Samaritan holy men refuse.

The Bible doesn't give us much other than the interaction between the disciples and their master, Jesus. But it is clear they don't seem very happy with the outcome, and they must have felt some fear preparing for whatever Jesus had in mind.

They didn't tell Jesus the situation in order to come to some sort of resolution. They didn't try to negotiate with the Samaritans. They simply drew the line between the two groups, and their version of success was to ask Jesus if He thought it was okay if they called down fire to destroy an entire people.

Can you imagine the fear and embarrassment Jesus must have felt when the disciples He was living with wanted to destroy another people group? There He was teaching people that "God so loved the world," and in a moment of veritable un-accomplishment, His disciples suggested fire and brimstone for the people who'd rejected their request for travel help. No wonder Jesus continued to use the phrase, "O you of little faith" (see Matt. 6:30; 8:26; 16:8; Luke 12:28).

In His frustration with His followers, Jesus responded in a way consistent with His earlier message. He didn't give in to the disciples' request. He wasn't going to let the mob mentality of tribalism distract Him from His message or the road to Jerusalem. He didn't even give it a moment's thought; He began rebuking the disciples' anger, defeat, and prideful insults.

I've read through this story thousands of times, and I usually identify myself as the one who can hear Jesus's message loud and clear. Of course I would be on the side of Jesus, because I'm *that good*, and I know I could have effected actual change with Jesus.

How silly am I? I never want to read the gospel message through a lens that equates me with those "idiot" disciples who don't know what they're doing. But if I'm honest with myself, I probably fear the same things they feared. I fear people who think I shouldn't include others on my spiritual journey. I fear people who scoff at God and invite judgment into their own lives. I fear what my own tribe would think of me if I spent any time fraternizing with the "enemy" or the "other." If I didn't, my life would look a lot different, right?

I would take time to worship in African American churches. I would embrace fellow Christian denominations who are worshiping the same Son of God I teach. I wouldn't be so concerned with what people thought of me. And I certainly wouldn't allow this "all or nothing" idea of truth to guide my own behavior.

Instead, I would love my neighbor, no matter who they are. I would live life with people where they are, comfortably, instead of trying to live life with people where I think they should be. I wouldn't concern myself with someone's behavior as much as I would be concerned about the circumstances that brought them to a place where they believe they are living right.

What would life look like if we began to think about the people group that most offends our own tribe and actually took the time to sit down with them and talk? Play? Worship? Or, most offensively, become friends with *them*?

Interestingly enough, Jesus not only rebukes His disciples but recalls this moment in His very next parable, which is probably the most quoted story in the Gospel of Luke.

The Good Samaritan

On one occasion an expert in the law stood up to test Jesus. "Teacher," he asked, "what must I do to inherit eternal life?"

"What is written in the Law?" he replied. "How do you read it?"

He answered, "'Love the Lord your God with all your heart and with all your soul and with all your strength and with all your mind'; and, 'Love your neighbor as yourself.'"

"You have answered correctly," Jesus replied. "Do this and you will live."

But he wanted to justify himself, so he asked Jesus, "And who is my neighbor?"

In reply Jesus said: "A man was going down from Jerusalem to Jericho, when he was attacked by robbers. They stripped him of his clothes, beat him and went away, leaving him half dead. A priest happened to be going down the same road, and when he saw the man, he passed by on the other side. So too, a Levite, when he came to the place and saw him, passed by on the other side. But a Samaritan, as he traveled, came where the man was; and when he saw him, he took pity on him. He went to him and bandaged his wounds, pouring on oil and wine. Then he put the man on his own donkey, brought him to an inn and took care of him. The next day he took out two denarii and gave them to the innkeeper. 'Look after him,' he said, 'and when I return, I will reimburse you for any extra expense you may have.'

"Which of these three do you think was a neighbor to the man who fell into the hands of robbers?"

The expert in the law replied, "The one who had mercy on him."

Jesus told him, "Go and do likewise." (Luke 10:25–37)

The significance of the story can't be overstated. Jesus had just rebuked his disciples in the previous chapter because they didn't want to have anything to do with the Samaritan people. So when a religious leader tries to trap Jesus with the "Who is my neighbor?" question, Jesus quickly introduces a Samaritan hero to the story. I wonder if the disciples got it?

Jesus probably looked over the shoulders of the religious leaders and caught Peter's eye when he gave all this compassionate behavior to the Samaritan. On further exploration, this parable isn't about people who help people on the side of the road, as many pastors would try to squeeze into a Sunday message.

No, this story is clearly about asking yourself who you are most afraid of. Who are you most contentious toward? Who is the person or group of people in your life who cause you to feel the most disdain?

The real message the parable of the Good Samaritan asks: Who do you hate?

Those are the people we should start identifying as *neighbor*.

Those are the ones with whom we need to start working through our own personal fears.

We need to begin to love like the Samaritan. We need to begin to love the political group we hate. We need to begin to love the homosexual. We need to begin to love the prisoner. We need to love the European, the South American, the African, and the Middle Easterner.

The social baggage we carry from our own history needs to be carefully unpacked, and we need to find a place where we can honestly stand before the Creator of all humanity and begin finding a gentle heart of compassion for people who look different than we do, talk differently than we do, or believe differently than we do.

The shout of response from our own tribe will be, "Don't be ashamed of the gospel!" and all the while, under the guise of group-think, we reserve our care and concern for those just . . . like . . . us.

But to be truly ashamed of the gospel would be to deny our God-given opportunity to reach out to someone who thinks differently. *Ashamed* means to create boxes where God's children live one way and the "other" lives differently.

"Don't be ashamed of the gospel" isn't a call to take a stand on the mountain of truth in ignorance and defiance, as we may be inclined to believe. It means that in our difference we make a statement of care and friendship only found through God's Spirit of aggressive, compassionate grace.

If we're really serious about learning how to stop fearing the "other" and work in a world where we can truly reach out and give hope to people around the globe, we have to stop and really think about what battle cries we are going to use when we engage others.

The Christianese language of old isn't profitable anymore. We need to find a new way of talking. The "warrior spirit" of protecting the gospel is a dying concept. We need to transform our idea of "warriors" from those who are willing to die for their faith to those who are willing to love others no matter what the cost.

4

Learning to Love from a Place of Common Thought

Be strong and courageous. Do not be afraid or terrified because of them, for the LORD your God goes with you; he will never leave you nor forsake you.

Deuteronomy 31:6

When I first met my wife, Jamie Jo, in college, I was instantly attracted to her ability to love the people she disagreed with most. She didn't judge students for their lifestyles. She didn't run to the corner and hide from homosexuals. She loved people where they were and for the potential she saw in them. She had a unique ability to stand firm in her own ideas without imposing those ideas on others.

We were sitting in class one morning when she leaned over and asked, "What are you doing for spring break?"

As I recall, my friends were all planning their beach get-aways, ski trips, and long journeys home to enjoy a couple of days away from the classroom. I had a few opportunities but hadn't solidified any plans at the time.

"I'm not sure. What do you have in mind?" I asked.

"Well, I'm going to Cambodia to a hospital dedication."

I have to stop there.

Some of you are wondering, *Cambodia? Who goes to Cambodia for spring break? Cancun? Maybe. But Cambodia? Really?*

Well, here is a brag on my lovely wife: when she was four-teen years old, she saw a picture, provided by a major relief agency, of a starving orphan in Cambodia, and she was deeply troubled. She went to her father, plopped the picture down on the counter, and demanded in her fourteen-year-old's sassy tone, "We have to do something about this."

As only a father can do, he began putting together ideas about how his daughter might be able to experience the beau-tiful journey of sacrifice for the good of someone else. He took her interest for teenage fashion and coupled it together with a heart to love people in a foreign land in order to form a business, and in 1989 they opened a teen clothing company called White Sands.

For the next five years, Jamie Jo and her father waded through the shark-infested retail waters to build a company where teenagers could buy trendy clothes for a good price. They, in turn, donated a large portion of the profits to the relief agency to provide for the basic needs of Cambodian children. After nearly a decade, they had made enough to fund an entire pediatric hospital in the downtown part of the capital city, Phnom Penh.

So when I first met Jamie Jo as a college freshman, she was already thinking about how to fund big dreams. I was just trying to make it through biology so I could enjoy some spring break time on the beach with other college friends, and she was thinking globally. I liked her right from the start.

After a few conversations with my parents, they agreed to let me hop on a plane with her and fly to this remote nation. (Remember, this was well before the internet, cell phones, and Skype, so communication was extremely difficult.) At the time, Cambodia was still reeling from the Khmer Rouge regime that had slaughtered as many as three million citizens in order to implement communism in the 1970s.

I was about to see things few people outside this small Eastern country would ever see. We traveled through Bangkok, Thailand, and the first recollection I have is seeing grand statues of Buddha.

At the time, I hadn't explored any other faiths except the strict right-winged conservative culture I was used to. So you can imagine what I must have felt like, coming to Cambodia from a culture ready and willing to condemn anyone who would bow down to an idol.

I saw mothers worshiping while they lit incense to dead relatives. I saw grand pagodas erected to house monks living the simple life. I even visited a place called the Temple of 10,000 Buddhas. It was here in the Far East I remembered the movie *The Wizard of Oz*, thinking and wondering out loud, "I'm not in Kansas anymore."

What would God think of this godless land?

We arrived in Cambodia, and after a couple of days of overcoming jetlag we were well on our way to seeing the hospital my future wife had spent years funding from thousands of miles away.

Driving through the capital city was a tour of a war-torn area. Bomb craters riddled the streets, people missing limbs were begging on the corners, and worshipers visited beautiful temples to try to find some sort of meaning in life.

Talk about feeling unworthy. And evidently Jamie Jo was something of a celebrity. The tour of the hospital was more like a dedication, presented by none other than the president of Cambodia.

So here I was, outside the realm of most American college students, sitting in the presence of ministers and kings. I was also smack dab in the middle of fear.

After the dedication, we toured the hospital and got a chance to see various other projects in need of funding. I even got a chance to share devotions with the Cambodian Relief staff, the ones who were working to operate the various charities the agency was funding. They had people on the ground helping women who had been traded in sex trafficking schemes, schools where HIV positive kids lived, and camps teaching trades to people interested in getting back to work.

I'd never seen such love given away without any expectation for return. I was intrigued to learn more about the people willing to sacrifice their own lives for the good of others.

While we were on the other side of the world, we decided to extend our trip a bit for the purpose of "education." You know how that mission trip stuff works. You go for the mission, and then a little mission-cation on the side. On one of our trips I met a young man giving a tour of the ancient city Angkor Wat. The sprawling city was built in the northern region of Cambodia by the Hindus of the twelfth century and is considered one of the largest religious monuments in the world. The young tour guide was thorough in his teaching, and I learned a great deal about ancient Hinduism and the siege by Buddhists in the following centuries.

We got to one of the massive frescoes carved into the stone walls where a depiction of Hindu heaven told the story of the afterlife. The top of the wall depicted people playing, enjoying life, partying with family, and having a great time. Below, etched in the rock, were scenes of skeletons with wheelbarrows wheeling the dead to a great fire.

"Is that heaven and hell?" I asked.

"Yes," he replied. "After you live a good life, Vishnu decides whether you go to heaven or hell. Obviously you want to be sure you live a life of virtue, because that life"—he pointed to the hell portion—"is the place of eternal damnation."

We talked back and forth for nearly twenty minutes about the afterlife before I had a chance to talk about my own view of heaven and hell. I told him about the faith I held dear to my own heart and outlined the way Jesus came to reconcile the sinful people of earth to God the Father in heaven. We talked for what seemed like hours, and I found a vibrant new friendship emerging.

I learned how the universe was created out of Vishnu's mouth. I learned the role the Brahman plays in reincarnation. I explored the idea of behavior and what the meaning of life really was. He was such a gentle teacher, and I was an interested student.

As our conversation was nearing a close, he looked me deep in the eyes and said, "Andy, I must admit, I've never met any Christians like you."

"What do you mean?"

"So many Christians have come to Angkor Wat and tried to convert me to their brand of religion. You never once asked me to pray a prayer or leave my life and my family traditions. You didn't tell me I was going to hell, and you seemed interested in my life. Thank you."

I didn't really know how to respond.

Should I open my Bible to the Romans road and complete the sales pitch I had been taught in those thousands of hours of evangelism training? Had I failed my new friend? Or was I learning what it meant to simply *be* Jesus to people who don't know Him?

It was interesting for me to sit with my new friend and just soak up the information he thought was true and right.

I wasn't putting on any show for him or trying to patronize him while I waited for my chance to reveal "the one true gospel." I didn't try to use evangelism techniques Christians often attempt to conjure up to prove their commitment to the gospel.

I just listened.

And here we were, in a place where he was practically begging me for more information about this God and the Jesus I loved so dearly. I couldn't help but translate this moment into the work I would later do with high school and university students.

So often we think of God as a sales pitch. If we have the right information and say the right things at the right times, then people will "convert" and pray a prayer. Somewhere in our subconscious we think we're performing well for God, making sure we make Him proud without thinking about people as *people*.

And I get it.

With nearly two billion people on the planet worshiping idols many in the Christian world would find offensive, I am simply proposing that humanity is the same across the borders of country and culture.

Most everyone wants to figure out the true meaning of life. Most of us want to get a job that can provide for our families. We want our kids to be educated. We all want our lives to be significant in whatever ways our culture deems are important.

Nobody wakes up and says, "I can't wait to worship something that doesn't make any sense."

Nobody in their right mind says, "I know there's a *real* god out there, but I'm going to do my best with this idol right here in front of me."

The questions of human existence in every culture, every religion, and every place where people are breathing today are basically the same. So what's our responsibility?

Don't Be Afraid

After years of "world religions" Sunday school class, I was living in a world where there was one right way, and everyone else was just, well . . . *wrong*.

I could list all the religions of the world and provide the reasons why they didn't work, never taking into account the sheer number of people who adhered to these religions and who were doing the very best they knew to understand the human condition.

While this education was meant to give me confidence in what I believed in the face of those "other" people, something strange took place. Instead of helping me understand why following Jesus was important in lieu of all the other religions, these classes produced fear in my heart of anyone who thought differently than I did. *They* were "obviously" in the wrong, and I had to make a choice: either approach them with an agenda of conversion because I wanted to see them in heaven so badly, or try to distinguish them as different by culture, tradition, or religious norms.

I know the intention of the class was well meaning, but the result was just awful.

Some people can compartmentalize their faith in such a way as to make sense of this world, but if we're honest, it only tends to create this ugly "us versus them" narrative.

We see "those people" on the wrong team and "us" on the morally right team. But we forget, in the middle of the conflict, that *the game* is the core lesson. We tend to take sides and justify our positions, but when looked at from a different angle, someone else may have just the same preconception.

For example, we have all the answers, and they have all the problems.

For me, this was a totally mind-bending activity, and I still carry the psychological baggage around with me to this day. When I enter into a space where people are obviously different than I am, I begin making mental notes on why I'm right and they're wrong.

They don't worship like I do.

They don't dress like I do.

They don't smell like I do.

They don't lead like I do.

They don't operate the same way I do.

But instead of looking at the world through the lens of "us versus them," maybe it's time we started looking at the world through the lens of "God created every man, woman, and child, and they are all special to Him." I'm not advocating some sort of pseudo-universalism here. I'm only trying to explore the possibility that many in the world are trying, with the best of intentions, to figure out how in the world they can make sense of God.

When I told my Hindu friend about Jesus, his eyes lit up, and you could see his hunger to know a God who loves all humankind. It was an unbelievable experience to sense how living like Jesus works in the real world, without trying to sell God to someone else.

Don't Be Weird

Christians are renowned for being a strange tribe. We have our own language, our own subculture, and at least in Western Christian groups we think we have the answer for everyone else in the world.

If they only believed in Jesus, then they would be better off in life.

I, for one, think we spend entirely too much time trying to live other people's lives for them, instead of approaching our knowledge with a simple humility.

We think we need to defend God, convert people, and bring them to a place of confession.

Well . . . maybe.

What if God just wants us to walk like Jesus did?

He walked into the homes of people who distorted the greatest message of all time. He gave time to the spiritually bankrupt in order to show them how to live. He put a high value on taking care of someone's physical needs and, as in the story with my Buddhist friend, their need to be heard.

As a young church attendee, I was encouraged to be a "Jesus Freak." And to be honest, the only good that did was to encourage me to be a part of a tribe of other Jesus Freaks.

The world didn't care that I chose to live my life differently. I never heard any comments on the cheesy T-shirts I wore outside the church. It was really only other Christians who were impressed with my weirdness.

When I decided to live in the world and stop being so strange, people started coming to me asking questions about faith, rather than me trying to garner up some sort of interest in godly questions.

It's a simple concept: just don't be weird.

Unless, of course, *weird* includes caring for people who are trying to understand life like you are, are striving for some form of hope, or maybe just need to express themselves as, well . . . people.

Listen Well

Too often we're taught that we have to talk. We have to fill the space of conversation with our knowledge of the gospel.

Too few of us, however, are students of *listening*.

The beauty of learning to love my Buddhist friend wasn't that I could outthink, out-defend, or out-argue him. No, the beauty of my new friendship was the fact I had a chance to just sit down and honestly be interested in his life. It's an amazing lesson concerning the human condition. We all want someone else to value us for who we are. It doesn't matter if we live in America, Cambodia, Spain, or China. Churning in the soul of every living person is a longing to be understood.

If we had a chance to check our fear of others at the door of conversation, we could start being students of listening well. We don't have to impose our thoughts and feelings on someone else. We can simply listen to whatever views they have, not as part of an agenda but just as a new way of seeing a beautiful, God-created human being.

To be honest, the comment "I've never met any Christians like you" is kind of my mantra now. Buddhists, Hindus, atheists, agnostics, and others from all forms of monotheistic faith have expressed this to me in one form or another.

I see it as a badge of honor as I try to follow Jesus the way He's called me to follow, and I want to be someone who draws the broad mystery of God to the table of conversation.

I promise you, it's nothing I really set out to do. It just happens. It happens because I'm not afraid of anyone else's ideas. I've sat with leaders of churches, mosques, and universities, and each time I try to listen well they all have the same response. They want to know why I believe what I do.

Most people can realize the effort it takes to actively listen to another, and they reciprocate the gesture. In a world spinning out of control and laced with more and more options, we find it rare to be able to slow down, look someone in the eye, and care deeply for their life story. So if you just want to connect with someone, take some time out and give them the most valuable commodity that you have on earth today, *your time.*

I wonder if that's what people thought of Jesus while He wandered the countryside showing compassion to all people, no matter where they came from. It was the time He gave, above anything else, that showed people they were valuable. It's amazing what can happen when you just engage with someone else with no agenda other than to listen.

Truth from Different Perspectives

I've spent a fair amount of time in the last decade with colleagues who call themselves "worldview teachers." They have creative arguments that help differentiate between different ways of seeing the world, and they help each student to identify the ways their particular worldview is right.

When engaging in the *worldview world*, the lines of black and white become clear. Each organization tries to educate people right down the lines of how they think the world should spin. As a young student of Christian worldview thinking, I was caught up in the "this is right, that is wrong" mentality. But the truth of the matter is, even though there are certainly ideas in the world that are clear-cut black and white issues, with seven billion people on the planet we have an obligation to explore some of the gray ones too.

When the study of "the Christian worldview" began gaining steam in the halls of church laypeople, words like *relativism*, *situational ethics*, and *postmodern* became the battleground for the Christian culture. These were the *evil* words that no one in the class wanted to adopt. In fact, there was no room for people to even think through how these ideas would mold and shape a generation.

And at the same time, the culture was adopting these words as real parts of existence. One prominent worldview thinker told me, "We must fight for the ideas of absolute truth or else our way of living will decay into the Wild West of ethical thinking."

In that particular moment in my young ideology, I adopted his philosophy.

Everywhere I spoke to groups about worldview, I made sure to posit absolute truth with every other type of thinking so we could recognize the ideas that were *most right*. The thinking was, if we could engage people at an intellectual level they would come to a place of understanding where there is only one way to think, and that's "God's way." In essence, we were the warriors fighting the battle of academia, minimizing the way the culture was moving.

The problem in thinking through the absolute truth argument is you leave an entire culture in the wake of your black and white thinking. I happen to agree there are moral ethics that work well, as the Creator of the universe outlined how life works on Planet Earth, but when we take such an absolute stance we begin to alienate that planet's population. (I can already hear the cries of my former teachers who are reading this.) I'm not proposing there aren't absolute ways of thinking about morality. What I am proposing is how we practically approach the culture in those ideas.

The God Question

One of the most crucial questions we must establish when thinking about worldview is the character and nature of God. When we ask students and young adults about their own perspectives of who God is and how God functions in the world today, we get as many answers as there are students in the class.

Some believe God is a friend. Some believe God is a judge. Some believe God is unreachable. Some believe God is the old man CEO sitting on the throne of heaven, ready to strike them down.

So we have an obligation to engage in the question, "Who is God?" And an even more troubling question to the worldview advocates: "Is there even a God in the universe at all? How do you know?"

I was one of those students teachers love to have in their classroom. I read every word in the books they assigned, attended every lecture, spent time well into the night discussing concepts with my friends, and cruised through with a high grade point average. I made a lot of friends among my teachers in both high school and college.

When I was a freshman in college, one of the classes I looked forward to the most was philosophy. I learned early that my gift was not in math or science. The questions I asked at the university level had more to do with *why* we were here rather than *what* we were.

So when I was in anatomy class dissecting frogs, I didn't care much to describe what was inside the frog as much as I cared to ask, "Why are there frogs in the world anyway?"

Philosophy has a unique way of calling a person to the most intimate *whys* of life. Why do we know? Why do we think? How can we articulate ethical moral questions?

Ancient philosophers such as Socrates, Aristotle, and Plato set a foundation for Western thinking and education. So when I entered my Intro to Philosophy class with books in tow I felt like I was going to be intellectually mentored by the greats. I was ready for the professor to share with me the wisdom of life as seen through the eyes of the great thinkers of the world.

When my professor took the podium, he didn't start with the ancient Greeks or even the modern thinkers like Nietzsche or Kierkegaard. He started by asking a few simple questions that began to deconstruct the reality I'd known to that point.

"Class, how do you know the sky is blue? Prove it," he posited.

"Well, we can see it," one student answered.

"Someone told us it was blue," another piped up.

"We know blue by the light waves we study in physical science." The scientist sat back proudly as he thought he'd answered correctly.

"How do you know it's not green and society hasn't just conditioned you to call it blue?" the professor asked. The class was silent.

"I guess . . . well . . . we don't know," another student answered sheepishly.

And I started thinking. *If my mom told me the sky was blue . . . and I couldn't prove the sky was blue . . . the philosophy professor told me I don't know . . . then what color is it?*

The next question he asked was, "How do you know you're alive? Prove it."

"Our hearts are beating," one student chimed in.

"We're breathing," said another.

"I think, therefore I am." The philosopher of the group tried to suck up to the teacher.

"Does your heart beat when you're dreaming?" the professor retorted. "Do you breathe when you dream? Do you think when you're dreaming?"

We all nodded our heads in agreement.

"Then how do you know you're not a butterfly in Africa dreaming you're a human sitting in my class right now?"

Boom! My brain exploded. I had never heard anything like this before. *If my mom told me the sky was blue, and now it may not be . . . if my mom told me I was alive and now that's negotiable . . . then what can I know to be true?* I took the questions to their natural end games.

How did I know I was going to the right church? How did I know church was even something I needed to do? How did I know the Bible was true? Or better yet, how did I know there was even a God in the universe at all?

For many of us from evangelical backgrounds, we don't even question the existence of God. If you took a survey of your average church-attending parishioner, I think you'd be surprised how many believe in something they've never thought through before. Go ahead, try it.

Different Views of God

With seven billion people in the world, there are some who believe there is some sort of God, some who believe in lots of gods, and others who claim there is no way there is a God in the universe at all. We live in a world where we can connect in an instant with people from around the globe who have various opinions of how God works—or doesn't—in the universe. And what this connection does is call us to think about how we interact with people who don't think like us.

Crazy as it may sound, atheists aren't demonic. Hindus are real people trying to figure out how to interact on a spiritual plane. Buddhists are people trying to find meaning through overcoming suffering. Muslims are devoted to One God. Jews are real people finding devotion as a pinnacle of their own spiritual existence. And Christians . . . well, there are over 3,500 different views and denominations out there.

Again, don't try to label me as a Universalist. I'm only trying to help my tribe, the evangelical tribe, understand how the world really spins and how we can engage all these different types of people. If we simply stand on the pinnacle of truth without any regard for anyone else's way of thinking, we will continue to isolate our tradition. We'll start drawing lines of right and wrong so definitively that we'll leave the other six billion people on the planet lost in the wake of our preaching methodology.

Fear drives us to the shadows of ignorance.

Fear makes us hold on to what we know and what we know works.

Fear doesn't allow for us to engage in new environments with people who think differently than we do. But if we can humbly approach our relationships while intentionally learning how to communicate what we think is right and wrong, the space of conversation becomes much more intriguing. And who knows, we might be able to learn something new along the way too.

5

Eliminating Fear
by Following Jesus

David also said to Solomon his son, "Be strong and courageous, and do the work. Do not be afraid or discouraged,
for the LORD God, my God, is with you. He will not fail you or
forsake you until all the work for the service of the temple of
the LORD is finished."

1 Chronicles 28:20

WWJD. Remember that Christian campaign? Sometime in
the early '90s, a campaign began inside the Christian community to ask ourselves "What would Jesus do?" WWJD.

There were bracelets, books, and bumper stickers to give
people a clear reference point for those who wanted to follow
Jesus. If you wore a WWJD bracelet, whenever you looked
down at your wrist you would ask yourself if Jesus would be
doing whatever it was you were doing. If you had a WWJD
bumper sticker, the intent was that everywhere you drove

you would have some accountability to ask yourself, *Would Jesus be doing this?* We had constant reminders all around us to align our thoughts, our behavior, and our dealings with others with what Jesus would do if He were in our place.

I thought it was an incredible idea at the time. The people who came up with the movement were spot on. But, like all other such programs in our lives, it eventually lost its luster and began to be more of a duty than a lifestyle change.

It is my deepest heart's desire to follow Jesus with an honesty and integrity that match His. As a follower of Jesus, I don't simply want to participate in cultural norms but to have the ability to ask hard questions about how He wants me to live in the world. This includes the areas of fear invading my ideas of what is right and what is wrong.

I often wonder what Jesus did when He was scared of another, was isolated from a particular group, or had to face life when it didn't turn out like He wanted.

The Garden of Jesus and the Sharing of Suffering

In October 2013, I traveled to Israel. I was traveling with a group from America working with high-profile leaders in the region concerning the Israeli/Palestinian conflict.

We began our journey in Beirut, talking with Palestinian refugees who were living on the border, and then our journey led to Jordan. We decided it would be easier to cross into Israel from Amman, Jordan, than from the heavily secured Lebanese border.

We got on the bus on the Jordanian side of the checkpoint and found the drop-off point where we had to get off and wait for the Israeli bus to come and pick us up. We were traveling with a mostly Arab constituency at this point, and the air was thick with suspicion. It felt like everyone we talked with was looking out for some sort of security risk. I guess when you live in a region that is in constant war with little to no hope of peace there are few places to find solace.

After we crossed the border we entered security and border control. Everyone treated us with the utmost dignity, and when I walked outside, for the first time in my life, I was actually standing on the land spoken of in the Bible. Previously, I never really had much interest in going to the Holy Land. And I have to admit, on first glance I wondered, *Is this really the Promised Land? God must have forgotten He created Colorado!*

Our first adventure was to go to the Jordan River where Jesus was baptized. (At least, they said it was the place where He *may* have been baptized.) We walked in, paid a fee, and then walked through a gift shop full of oils, soaps, and Jesus trinkets. It was like a Disney World of Jesus, of sorts.

We then made our way down to where the lush green branches hung over the clear water of the Jordan. People dressed in white linen were standing in line waiting for their chance to fulfill their dreams and hopes in obedience to their Savior. I sat and watched for hours as these spiritual journeymen arrived at their first destination of a Holy Land tour. Each time someone came out of the water, their face glowed as if God Himself had touched their body. It was deeply emotional for all involved, and for my people watching the tour that day it was a great spiritual encouragement. I was moved to tears on more than one occasion, seeing people drown their old lives in the river to rise up believing they were now brand-new. It was the ultimate view of hope.

As we finished our time at the river, the sunset over the Jordan River valley was majestic. It seemed so surreal to be walking where Jesus walked and to see this immaculate picture of the sun setting over Bethlehem. Then we had to catch some sleep and prepare for our big day traveling through Jerusalem.

When the sun came up, we grabbed a quick breakfast and went on our way. The beginning of our journey was viewing the Temple Mount. You know that picture seen in all the Dome of the Rock pictures? We visited as normal tourists and then found a long, winding road down to the Garden of Gethsemane.

The Garden of Gethsemane represents ultimate pain to those of us who believe the gospel story. Gethsemane is a place where olive trees make up a large part of the local economy. The word *gethsemane* refers to the place where the olive press would actually crush the olives to produce olive oil, a major commodity in the region. It's no wonder this was the place where Jesus sweat blood in agony over what was about to happen. He was literally feeling the spiritual press as God had destined Him to go to the cross. "Father, if you are willing, take this cup from me; yet not my will, but yours be done" (Luke 22:42).

He begged God the Father to rethink the road to one of the most excruciating capital punishments ever invented. And here I was, sitting among some of the same trees that had given shade to the Son of God before His death.

I approached the resident chaplain of our trip and asked if he would lead us in a prayer and meditation exercise. He agreed. We gathered together around an old olive tree. One of the tour guides told us this tree was dated to be nearly two thousand years old. If this garden was truly the place where

Jesus grieved, then I was sitting under branches touched by the divine. This was the closest I'd ever come to touching the very garments of God. And in the moment, I began to feel the immense suffering Jesus talked about in the Gospels.

I also felt the distractions all of the disciples must have felt, and then in a single moment, I felt the question that plagues most of humanity. Mainly, *Why?* Why is there pain and suffering in the world today? If God is truly as good as we claim Him to be, why does He allow it? Couldn't the big, all-powerful, all-loving God do away with the suffering we all go through? If He doesn't, then does He really love us? I can't imagine imposing suffering on my children. I have five wonderful kids, and if any one of them came to me and begged for relief from whatever suffering they were going through, I would do everything in my power to reach out and help.

Here in the Garden, I learned a few things about the fear of pain and suffering.

The fear of suffering overshadows much of what we were meant to accomplish in the world.

Imagine if Jesus had backed out of the walk to Golgotha. What if He'd decided it was too tough?

Or what if He'd looked to the heavens in belief that God's plan for His life was laced with nothing but success and goodness? What if Jesus had believed that kingship here on earth was His destiny, and to be crucified on a cross made no sense at all?

He knew and harbored one clear fact of life: that fear, pain, and suffering accompany much of what God uses to accomplish great things.

The modern-day understanding of God's blessing is centered around the idea that if we accept and choose to follow Jesus, life is going to be better. He is poised and ready to bless our business financially, take away all the pain of family struggles, or even make life smoother. But that's just not the case. Every character in the Bible was carefully written about to give us examples of pain. Why do we think we have something that might make us better than Moses, Abraham, David, Paul, or the apostle John? There's nothing special about our being born in the world two thousand years after Jesus walked the planet.

The human condition is plagued by pain and suffering. So instead of asking the question, "Why does God allow evil to happen?" maybe the question should be, "How could I engage with God's story in the middle of what He's trying to do, in order that I might honestly approach life 'counting it pure joy to endure trials of many kinds'?"

This doesn't mean the darkness has to be a place of happiness. This doesn't mean it's going to be fun. But what this approach does encourage us to do is welcome and honestly deal with the fear that may creep into our hearts as we live in a world that sensationalizes tragedy and bad news.

We don't have to create spaces of safety. Jesus never taught that life was going to be safe, clean, and without pain. In fact, He continually encourages those who follow Him to:

Take up our cross (Luke 9:23).

Be ready when the world threatens us (1 Pet. 3:15).

Understand the temptation to deny our walk with Him (Matt. 4:1–11).

Be encouraged, for He will never leave us or forsake us (Heb. 13:5–6).

We can never live "an abundant life" without facing our fears head-on.

A few years ago, I was introduced to a pastor who had a few home churches that met on their own every other Sunday, and on the Sundays in between they met together at a country club. All were welcome. None were shunned. All were encouraged to be honest in their faith journey.

The first meeting I had with this home church, the people introduced themselves before the teaching part of the meeting. One lady introduced herself and shared, "I'm working through the pain of having chosen an abortion when I was in my twenties."

I thought that was a little strange, but it was refreshing that she was courageous enough to bring her pain to the group.

The next guy shared, "I'm dealing with the addiction to perform. I feel like I'm always trying to think of what's best for me, instead of allowing God's Spirit to guide and direct me."

Again, I thought this was a little strange, but okay . . .

Next, a mother shared, "I grew up in a very heavily sexualized family. I remember orgy parties my father took me to, and I'm learning to overcome a poor image of sexuality as I grow in understanding God's will for my life."

I sat with my jaw open, not even aware of my reaction at first. I'd never seen a group of people so honest with one another without *years* of relational development. They welcomed me into their pain even though I didn't have any reason to give them any of my own history of pain and suffering. I had to know what was going on here, so I scheduled a meeting with the pastor.

His name was Bob, and I now know what everyone else there knew. From the day we met, I called Bob my spiritual Jedi master, because he understood the key to growing out of our rut to a place of spiritual abundance. When we met in the living room of another friend's home, Bob casually asked, "So why are we meeting here today?"

"I just don't know what's going on here. Everywhere I go it seems the message of the church is pretty calculated. Follow Jesus plus manage your own sin equals blessing. But I've never seen a group so honest and willing to face their fears and their pain as I did in your church. They don't have any games to play here."

Bob smiled. "Andy, the key to growing in your own spiritual formation is to encounter Jesus in the fear and the pain your life has served. We all have specific moments in our lives that change our trajectory, and most of us just try to hide it and move on. But what happens is that point of fear becomes the place we make every life decision."

And I started to understand what he was saying.

Bob invited me to participate in what he calls "inner healing," a mix of psychology, counseling, and spiritual formation. We talked about the time in my life when I found myself most scared, rejected, and lonely. After about an hour, Bob looked at me and asked, "What would happen if Jesus entered the room in the very moment you felt the most fear?"

"I think He would walk over to me, put His arm around me, and say, 'I'm with you.'"

And something happened right in that very moment.

I believed.

I believed Jesus loved me.

I believed He was in my corner.

I knew, in the depth of my own soul, that Jesus was more than a first-century revolutionary. He was full of kingdom-deserved power.

He cared about me.

When I tell this story to my friends they think I'm crazy. But they can't take away my own personal experience of knowing God *does* care about my suffering, and that doesn't mean He's some sort of genie there to prevent me from going through it.

The pain Jesus endured in the garden was the pinnacle of self-denial.

As Jesus sweat blood, surely He understood the physical pain awaiting Him.

He knew what it was going to take to accomplish the mission God gave Him. He understood the physical pain He was about to endure, the spiritual pain of being alone on the cross, and the social pain from all His friends' rejection, and He did it anyway. Jesus understood His own self-preservation wasn't the most important part of God's redemptive plan.

As we follow Jesus, we must put on similar clothes of self-denial. Much of our fear surrounding faith has to do with protecting our own image, our own sense of right and wrong, or even more our own faith and sense of righteousness. It didn't make any sense to the people who followed Jesus that He would walk the lonely road to death. It didn't seem to fit the narrative. Jesus had acquired quite a following while teaching about the kingdom of God. I believe the tears He shed were due in part to the fact He was about to sacrifice the ministry momentum He had built for the sake of the bigger picture.

I run into people all the time who are more interested in being a role model for God than in taking on a spirit of humility, denying their own personal agenda for the good of the whole.

We are terribly afraid to sacrifice ourselves in order to see God's plan take root. If we're honest, we believe God needs us to continue doing whatever is working rather than sometimes listening intently to His command of self-sacrifice.

———◆———

How does a pastor approach a congregation that is longing for a "perfect leader"? We all know pastors struggle with the same human condition we all have to deal with, but somewhere along the way we give them the platform of perfection. How does a father sacrifice the cultural need to be a "good dad" in order to listen to God's potential plan for his kids to know Him in a more intimate way that may only be achieved by facing their biggest fears? How does a mother look into the face of her social group, admit the failures of her kids, and find the sense of togetherness God calls us to?

Jesus's struggle in the Garden is an important lesson for those of us looking to find blessing from God in the face of adversity. I think it's important we suffer through the Garden of Gethsemane with Jesus. We need to understand the God-man who knew the pain of His coming days but had faith God was still on the throne.

So what we are so afraid of?

WHEN WORLDVIEWS
Collide

6

On One Side There's a Mormon and on the Other Side There's a Jehovah's Witness . . .

When I am afraid, I put my trust in you. In God, whose word I praise—in God I trust and am not afraid. What can mere mortals do to me?

Psalm 56:3-4

In the conservative church I grew up in, I took a class on world religions and cults. Learning how Mormons, Jehovah's Witnesses, and Scientologists were all out to convert me to their view created skepticism in my worldview whenever I encountered my neighbors. What does an evangelical do when a Mormon comes knocking on their door? How do I talk with a Jehovah's Witness? And what exactly is the Scientologists' method of converting me?

Several teachers tried to use the counterfeit argument to prepare me for the onslaught of all these people who were out to get me. But instead of instilling confidence in my own faith, they actually created this cloud of fear in me when I saw a couple of guys dressed in white shirts pull their bikes up to my parents' front door. (I'm assuming we've all seen the missionaries out talking about their faith.)

In my own home it first happened when a small white minivan pulled in the driveway. I was in the basement far from the action, ignorant of what was going on upstairs, when I heard the doorbell ring. Jamie Jo went to answer the door, and then I heard the basement door open to her calling, "Andy, you have visitors."

It's amazing to me how my wife, who loves conflict, is so quick to pawn off the religious zealots on the worldview maestro.

Intrigued, as I wasn't expecting any visitors, I walked up and quickly took in the situation. There was a lanky teenager standing in the doorway dressed in khaki pants and a button-down shirt. His tie was cocked to the right, and he held a pamphlet in his hand. I saw the title of his little book held in front of him, and I immediately recognized the game that was afoot. I decided to test this young man and see how the conversation would play out.

"Can I help you?" I asked innocently.

"I was just . . . ahhh . . . wondering . . . ahhh . . . if you have ever . . . ahhh . . . thought about the coming endtimes." He stuttered through his first line.

I laughed audibly and quickly tried to catch myself so as to not come across as rude. "Well, actually, I'm pretty interested in how the world is going to end," I offered as bait.

He passed me the comic book pamphlet he was holding, and I immediately noticed the label "The Watchtower." Because of my studies in world religions, I pegged him as our neighborhood Jehovah's Witness missionary.

"I tell you what, why don't you come on in and sit down. It's hot out there, and I'd love to get you something to drink. You okay with that?" I asked the young apostle. With sweat pouring down his face, he cracked a smile and agreed. We walked into my small living room, and I poured us each a glass of iced tea. He gulped it down like a starving orphan and smiled politely. "I guess I was thirsty."

We laughed together as I reached for the tea container to pour another glass. "So tell me about this end of the world stuff," I said.

And so it began.

He told me how God was the Creator of the world and was ready to judge it. He told me about how there would be people selected to be saved, but most of us were going to perish. He asked me politely if I would ever consider following God, and then there was another knock at the door. Evidently, he was with a team and had left them sitting in the little white minivan in the driveway, consumed by the summer heat. We opened the door, invited them in, and now there were three adult leaders of the Jehovah's Witness church sitting in my living room.

"You guys okay?" I asked.

The senior statesman of the group replied, "It's just so hot out there. Would you mind if we come to join the conversation?"

"Of course, my home is your home." And as I turned to get more cups, my lovely wife was already serving up three fresh iced tea glasses.

"Here, take this," I insisted.

All three drank as though they hadn't had any water for months. I wondered, *Did any of my neighbors invite them in, or did they take the cues from our old cult classes and just shut the door?*

We talked for hours about the beginning of the world, the place for God, and their delusions about who Jesus was, at least according to my evangelical background. They made their case, and in the middle I stopped them.

"I really like you guys. I'm impressed you'd take to the street on such a hot day, knocking from door to door. Would you all like to have dinner with us tonight, and we can discuss our differences together some more then?"

They looked at each other like an alien had just touched down.

"Well, I guess we don't have any appointments this evening." They smiled in agreement.

"Great!" I said. "You guys can come back and try to convert me tonight. And in the meantime, we'll cook up an awesome dinner fit for a king."

We all laughed. They knew I must have had some experience, and I let the tension out of the room by calling their agenda to the table.

They came over that night. We had a delightful meal. I learned so much about the belief system that drove them from house to house. And when it was over I saw them to the door.

"Hey guys, I'm really thankful you came by today. I've never been so respected by someone who thinks so differently than I do," I said. "I just want you to know, I hope we can continue talking about this as our friendship grows."

Our conversations lasted for nearly a year. Back and forth, asking questions, listening to one another, trying to figure out where the other group was coming from, I learned so much from these friends. Mostly, they were all trying to make a living elsewhere, someone in their church had sent them out to fulfil some kind of mission, and they had similar baggage to mine. All of them were looking at the world through the prism in which God had shown up to them.

It wasn't long before their deacon came over, and then a few weeks later their pastor, and finally their whole board of directors came to discuss God with this recovering evangelical pastor. They were intrigued that I never brought up hell or damnation, or tried to convert them, but I was quick to point out when I thought they were trying to work on me. I often would say things like, "Come on . . . not the sales pitch again. Our conversations are more than that." They would laugh, and we'd just keep doing what we were doing.

We worked through pain and suffering.

We talked of the divinity of Jesus.

We discovered similarities in our view of the Spirit who lives inside.

It was an amazing time, almost like I'd stepped into the real college experience without ever having to leave my home. And you know what I discovered? Even though I didn't agree with my new friends' theology, we had a lot of things in common. We all liked to watch football. A couple of the guys liked to fly fish, so I became the resident Orvis fly-fishing instructor. The ladies found a common place with my wife, who was raising kids and trying to work professionally. And in one epiphany, I thought, *We're really not that different.* Sure, we had different ideas as to how the Bible was written, who God was, and how Jesus's ultimate role in the endtimes was going to work out, but we were all just trying to make sense of the world around us. They weren't "those" people I had to be scared of, as my Sunday school teachers had tried to portray them; they were just people. This became a fundamental foundation for how I live my life.

I've had to go back and rethink some of the common phrases in my early Christian life that had helped to instill this fear of the "other." These phrases created a system of theology I'm still trying to get over. Here, I'll share a few of them, and maybe you can begin finding freedom in living with God in a real environment instead of conjuring up cute slogans.

"Don't Be Afraid of the Gospel"

All my life I was taught "don't be afraid of the gospel" in situations that call us to stand up for our faith. Obviously the verse used was Paul's declaration in Romans, "For I am not ashamed of the gospel, because it is the power of God that brings salvation to everyone who believes: first to the Jew, then to the Gentile" (Rom. 1:16).

As I reflect back on those formative years, I see this battle cry of not being ashamed of the gospel was used in a negative context. It was almost like the teachers and leaders claiming the mantra were somehow afraid that if enough people were scared to share their faith in a particular manner, then Christians all over the world would suffer. The number of believers would decline, and ultimately God wouldn't stand with you when you needed Him.

I understand the intentions, but as a young guy looking to make sure I was living right, this was a mind-bender for me. It felt like I had to make sure to prove my dedication to God by sharing every theological point I knew about Jesus, the Holy Spirit, and God the Father *all in one sitting.*

If I didn't share it with the waitress at dinner and the guy working behind the counter at the gas station, or if I even gave any credence to another sect of Christian living, somehow I was rejecting God. My Christian life was measured by how many times I shared my faith to the point at which someone would pray the sinner's prayer (which I later found out isn't in Scripture *anywhere*).

What a guilt trip I began to shoulder! Every day I would think to myself, *Was I ashamed of the gospel today at school? Did I share at work? What am I supposed to do with so and so in my life?* I became less of an ambassador for the gospel and more of a salesman for God. And if I didn't prove my unrelenting support of the methods being taught in my tribe, somehow I put myself on the outside.

When I started to see how God didn't demand theological perfection but rather clear devotion to listen to what He was teaching me, it was like I laid down the boulder of perfection and started to live *free.* I wasn't walking through life fearful of failure, and I started living in the moment.

As I began seeing people not as objects of my sales pitch but rather as people whom God cared for just like He cared for me, the whole world changed. I saw, through the eyes of others, how deeply God cared for me. He cared if my needs were met, just like I cared for people when I saw their needs.

He cared if I was anxious, just like my heart ached for those who were worried about how their life would play out. He called me to a life of piety, knowing I couldn't achieve it, and still loved me. And so I started living in a world where I could extend grace instead of judgment.

When I think back on "protecting the gospel," I often wonder what in the world I was trying to prove. And who was I trying to prove it to?

The biggest freedom is when you have the opportunity to share with people about God's rest. After all, it was Jesus who said, "My yoke is easy and my burden is light" (Matt. 11:30). But when we walk around carrying the duty of the gospel, it draws us into this guilt and shame narrative that raises the fear level in our lives. We are afraid someone won't go to heaven. We are afraid somehow we aren't being a good servant to God. We are afraid of being a failure in faith instead of living in the abundance of an easy yoke and a light burden.

We don't have to walk in fear of God but rather in humble obedience to what He's called us to be. I've found significant healing from my own fear since I let my "don't be afraid of the gospel" line fade into the history of my early faith years.

"We're in a Spiritual Battle That We Must Win"

Just because someone comes from a different place theologically doesn't mean they're trying to take over the world. Like I've mentioned before, most people in the world aren't trying to build an empire for themselves. They're trying to live according to the paradigm they've learned.

This paradigm comes from their family influence, the pressure from their friends, and the culture they choose to believe is right and true.

My Jehovah's Witness friends weren't trying to build an army. They truly cared for the world and the endtimes. They were concerned with the ultimate judgment they thought was coming, and their response was to go from door to door to make sure everyone they knew had a chance to opt out of the imminent suffering.

I hear pastors and teachers saying things like, "Be careful not to allow the Mormons and Jehovah's Witnesses into your house. That's their home turf, and if you let them in, you'll be subject to their lies." What a load of manipulation! I've learned the more someone needs to manipulate your actions in life, the more there is an air of fear clouding that relationship. They don't have the confidence that God exists in your home as well as out of your home. In reality they are calling you to set up barriers to people—people God wants to show truth to. People God loves.

I was amazed to find out my Jehovah's Witness friends didn't encounter any other home on my block willing to open the door. They went from house to house, and rejection was the norm. They didn't experience any care from my Christian neighbors. They just kept getting the door slammed in their faces.

It makes me sad to hear of Christians who proclaim God's undying universal sovereignty in the world and then hide behind theology as if that's going to be the answer to the world's most intimate human issues. We don't need any more information. We live in an information society. You can listen to the greatest pastors, teachers, and preachers with a simple internet search. You can download workbooks, be a part of Bible studies, and engage in the next series at your church, and all those things are well and good. But we all are swimming in a sea of noisy information, and what the world needs to see are people willing to be the hands and feet God has called us to be. They need to see people who are interested in knowing but who are also conditioned to translate knowledge into action.

What would it look like for you to welcome missionaries from another brand of religious fervor tomorrow? What if you didn't just walk by the Mormon table next time, thinking about the ways you're different, and instead started a friendship?

How would your Jehovah's Witness neighbors deal with you if you volunteered to help them move, got in the yard and helped them landscape, or invited them to an after-hours dinner with your coworkers?

I'm amazed how dispelling the fear of difference helps show people the authenticity of your theology. It doesn't have to be spoken all the time; it needs to be lived out.

"God Loves Those Who Love Themselves"

This brings me to a controversial section of this chapter. Somewhere in our Christian circles we began to think if we could out-argue the person on the subway, then we would win. Somewhere the word *apologetics* became less about how I might encourage my own faith and more about how I can arm myself to defend God.

Well, I've got news for you: if the God you serve needs you to defend Him, we're all in a world of hurt. God is God because, well, He doesn't need you to do anything for Him. I'll say it again: God doesn't need defending.

He asks for us, through the gospel, to enter in a reconciled relationship between humanity and the divine to help the world begin to spin the right direction. He doesn't need another argument concerning why suffering happens; He needs people to provide care and compassion in the middle of suffering. He doesn't need another hypothesis about how old the earth is; He needs people who find it amazing we are even on the planet to begin with. He doesn't need another $A + B = C$ argument; He only desires that we love Him with all that is inside us, and that we love our neighbor as ourselves (see Matt. 22:37–40).

Too many of us are scared to death to share our faith because we don't have our defense in place. We feel like we'll be rejected by our atheist friends, our agnostic friends, or those missionaries who knock on our front door. But what happens when we're willing to say, "I'm not sure about that. Let's find out together"?

I'll tell you what happens: a friendship emerges. You have a chance to work out your own thoughts on tough theological issues. You give space to your friends whom you care for. And, ultimately, you give God's job of moving in people's hearts back to God.

I started my faith journey thinking if I could only out-argue the critics there would be more people who couldn't help but fall in love with the God of the universe. Boy, was I wrong! The more I fought, the more resistance I met. The more I argued, the more arguments I got in. I don't know if I ever shared my faith through logic and then had someone say, "Hey, you're right. I'm a sinner and I need God to save me."

As I think about it, that happened a total of *zero* times. The people in your life don't want to know how much you know. They want to know how much you *care*. God rarely comes into the space of intellect to exalt us on the platform labeled, "Well, they've figured it out, so follow Me." Most people who come into an intimate relationship with the God of the universe tend to find faith intellectually stimulating but recognize their fundamental need for reconciliation on much more than just an intellectual level. Whether it's sin, pain, disease, or death, the gospel provides humanity the chance to re-up our relationship with God. We don't sit around arguing theology with God. After all . . . He's God.

So, no matter what missionary is knocking on your door, let me encourage you: a little hospitality goes a long way in knowing and showing people how much God loves you and them.

7

Dinner with Ronald McDonald and a Sunni Muslim

So do not fear, for I am with you; do not be dismayed, for I am
your God. I will strengthen you and help you; I will uphold you
with my righteous right hand.

Isaiah 41:10

In the last two decades fear has taken the spotlight on the
global stage. When terrorism is a part of our vocabulary as a
civilization, we have a duty to describe who "those people" are
and how to engage them. Some will try to be diplomats seeking relationships, while others will rush to violence and war.

Whether it's our discussions about dealing with extremism
in a post-9/11 world or a brief history lesson of the European
bus bombings on 7/11, sometimes we can be fearful of taking
any action to make the world a better place.

If we're not careful we can allow fear to dictate how we engage in the world going forward, and much of our fear is generated as we indulge in the media cycle of discouragement.

When I talk with people about terrorism in the world, they usually quote some news story they heard about the bad guys making the lives of the good guys miserable. I don't know about you, but I can't remember the last time I turned on the television and heard an uplifting story. We see more and more shooters in schools, governments threatening others, and even a complex dose of economic fear after the Great Recession of 2008–2012. It's like we have a drum constantly beating out its warning for us to watch out for someone behind us who is driven to impose harm in our lives.

In 2009, I was invited to be a speaker in an influential part of the Middle East. We boarded the plane in Washington, DC, and headed out to meet the friends who had asked me to present ideas about Christianity in a new world.

Our plane landed in Bahrain, and for the first time in my life the fear-baggage of terrorism started ringing loudly in my soul. You know, that baggage we all carry around from past experiences, media outlets, friends, or wherever you learned to think about a group different from you. We all carry that luggage through life. Some of it we packed intentionally, and some of it was packed for us. In any event, my metaphorical baggage was packed, and it began to appear out of nowhere.

I'm not proud of my first reaction, but I have to be honest. When I saw people speaking Arabic at a mosque, I wondered, *What hateful message are they spreading about America?* My initial reaction was totally unfounded and was a hodgepodge of all the negative press we hear in the West concerning the Middle East, but I didn't know any better. These people were a mix of "those" Muslims I'd learned about in my Sunday school class and the images of airplanes taking down buildings. I didn't know quite how to act, how to speak, or even how to approach someone with a covering on their head, even if it was accompanied by a smile.

Call me uneducated, or better yet, call me the majority of Americans today. We just don't know what to do with all the negative baggage we carry around with us when we travel the world.

My contact was a wonderful Indian man who greeted me at the baggage claim. "Hello, Mr. Braner, welcome to Bahrain. Have you ever been to the Middle East before?"

I didn't really have any reference for where to go from here, so I mustered up a friendly "thank you" and hurried on to the car.

"We have a little time before I take you to your first meeting. What would you like to see?"

"Well, I don't really know what's here," I replied. "What is something that is only here in Bahrain?"

"Oh sir, you must see the Grand Mosque. It is one of the most brilliant architectural buildings in this region."

Did I hear this guy right? Did he just say he was going to take me to a mosque? I thought through the groggy jetlag now pulsing through my brain.

"Umm, I'm not sure I should go to a mosque. I mean, am I even welcome there?"

"Oh, that's okay. I understand." He seemed to sense the uncomfortable attitude I was trying to hide. "I've got just the trip for you."

We spent the afternoon at one of the last remaining Christian/Muslim hospitals in the region. My driver was an executive at the health center and wanted to show me how Christians and Muslims could come together when the conversation was framed around healthcare.

When I walked into the emergency room, I didn't know what to do. There in the large waiting area were people of all nationalities. There were people dressed in an American style I could identify with, but there were also some people dressed in black abayas, some dressed in all blue and purple burqas, some with shoes, and some with barely enough clothes to be considered covered. It was a fusion of nations, all waiting for a doctor to take care of their physical needs.

We walked through the hospital and saw some cutting-edge technology, and then we made our way up to the CEO's office. The CEO was a brilliant man educated in America, a doctor for much of his career, and was more than hospitable in welcoming me to Bahrain and showing me some of his vision for this institution.

"We are trying to show the world that healthcare can be a centerpiece for reconciliation. It's funny how many people drop their religious ties when someone is sick," the CEO explained to me.

For the rest of the day I tried to understand how this man who claimed to follow Jesus was able to lay to rest all the baggage I was carrying toward certain people groups to minister to their physical needs. He claimed a unique place in my understanding of Jesus's message to love your neighbor no matter what.

After our tour through the hospital, my American friend came to pick me up and take me to my meeting. I got in the car and he said, "Well, I'm a bit early, anything you want to see? I think we have about an hour."

I thought for a split second. Facing my fear, I said, "I want to go to the mosque."

My First Tour through the Grand Mosque

"Are you crazy? I don't know if you noticed this, but you're in a Middle Eastern country now. This isn't America. You can't just march into the mosque and hang out with the Muslim worshipers. They take that stuff pretty seriously."

"Well, I'm here to talk about worldview, and I've got to be honest, I'm still trying to work through my own view of the world here."

"Okay." He winced sarcastically. "But I'm pretty sure they won't let us in," he said, trying to discourage me.

We pulled up to the Grand Mosque in Bahrain, a central place for Friday worship. He parked the car near the front of the enormous building, and I decided to get out and see what I could discover. My friend reluctantly followed, but he must have sensed the spirit of adventure I couldn't very well just leave at home. We walked up the great staircase and met a Muslim woman on her way out to the parking lot.

"Excuse me," I called out. "I'm wondering if it would be possible to take a tour of this beautiful building."

She looked at me through her local-style head covering, and in broken English said, "Come back later. It's closed."

As many of my friends will tell you, I do not get real excited about people saying something is not possible, so I persisted. "But I've come all the way from America, and I have to leave next Wednesday. This is my only chance to see your Grand Mosque."

Reluctantly she looked at me, sighed heavily, and turned around, waving me toward the front door. "Come. Come. I give you twenty minutes, but then you must leave."

I turned around to my American friend, shrugged my shoulders, and we walked toward the front door of the biggest building on the block. For the next hour and a half, this precious Arab woman showed me every nook and cranny of the Grand Mosque in Bahrain. She showed me the chandeliers flown in from France, the granite specially ordered from Italy, the artwork painted by local artisans, and when it was almost time to leave, she showed me how to pray.

"In the Muslim world we worship in special ways. We pray like this." She pulled out a laminated card of a man performing prayers in certain stages. "We believe when we fall down on our face before God we show our obedience and humility toward the Creator of the universe."

What? I've always been taught that your God is some sort of evil God that wants to kill everyone, I thought. But being respectful, I just smiled and listened.

"The imam stands over there to give his message after prayers," she kept explaining. I found her description of the worship performance fascinating. It's not that different from the way we worship, except for the different dress and a couple of action points.

"So, Mr. Braner, why are you so interested in Islam?" she asked at last.

The time had come. I didn't know how to respond without entering that place of extreme fear. *If I tell her I'm a Christian, am I doomed to be deported from the Middle East? If I don't tell her, am I ashamed of the gospel? What should I say?*

Before my thoughts caught up with my tongue, I blurted, "Well, I follow Jesus, and I think He'd want us to meet." She just looked at me with a blank stare of confusion. I thought, *I've really done it now.* She dropped her briefcase at my feet. I didn't know what was going to happen. Then she reached for my hands, a gesture reserved in the Middle East only for close friends, and she smiled.

"I'm glad you came here today. I've never met an American so interested in listening to how we do faith here in the Grand Mosque. Most just come to take pictures of the ornaments, but you, there's something different about you."

We talked for another hour. She gave me a suitcase full of materials explaining Islam. And on the way out the door she just kept thanking me for coming. I realized at that moment that all my fears about people who worshiped here in the Middle East needed a newfound, careful consideration.

Sure, there are bad people who wish to impose harm on others in the name of religion, but there are good people in the mix too. I sat in the backseat of the car on the drive to our meeting, which I was now two hours late for, and just began confessing. *God, I'm sorry I hold grudges against people I don't know. I'm sorry my heart is dark. Please forgive me for thinking people in this region are out to hurt me, You, and others. I hope there's a place here I can learn how to love people, even if I have to jump over my own hurdles of fear.*

And the trip carried on.

A Middle East Delicacy: McDonald's

About a year later, I brought my wife, Jamie Jo, back to the same place where I had met my doctor friend. She was amazed and delighted by the exceptional hospitality and safety. One night, my wife needed some good old-fashioned American food. The crazy part of the Middle East is that everywhere you look, American capitalism has taken over. Chili's is there, Macaroni Grill is there, and even our hometown favorite, McDonald's, is right there in the mall.

One of the most intriguing parts of courting my wife was the fact she was just as satisfied with a date to McDonald's as she was going to some fancy restaurant. And it doesn't take a rocket scientist to figure out you can get a meal for about five dollars at McDonald's and be just as full as you would be from a fifty-dollar steak dinner. So many of our dating meals happened right under the good old golden arches.

We found a McDonald's in the mall, and my wife was in heaven. Just a good old cheeseburger will do, she told me. As we were sitting at the table, we looked over to see a family of Sunni Muslims eating dinner. Two fathers, two mothers, and four kids running around the table made for a homelike feeling. I don't remember what we were talking about, but Jamie Jo leaned over to me and asked, "Why don't we ever see Muslim people like this?"

Here was a typical Muslim family enjoying a night out at the mall. Kids were running around acting like kids. Adults were engaged in their own conversations. One time I heard a mother scold a young child. And then I heard a father giving his children the encouraging news that they could go and play on the playground.

I examined our food court neighbors discreetly. After all, you don't want to look like a member of the NSA while you're hanging out in a sprawling Middle Eastern mall.

I watched and wondered.

It seems to me that most people in the world are trying to answer similar questions. They want to earn a good living. They want to raise their kids. They want to be doing what they consider is the right thing. But somewhere between "all humans are human" and "there are *those* people who are trying to take away the freedoms and principles I live in my own life," there's this great divide.

Sure, they dress a different way.

They speak a different language.

They pray differently.

They live in a country that is known for human rights issues.

But all in all, people are just *people*.

I wonder what it would take for us to see the world through the eyes of someone else and help create relationships where people can see God's love move through us. What would it look like to sit down and enjoy a meal with someone who lives in a world drastically different than your own? How many times are we willing to risk the fear of rejection, the fear of being seen with someone different, or the fear of having to change the ideas we hold so dear in our normal way of living?

Jesus did it—often. The Gospel of Matthew tells of people asking John the Baptist if Jesus was the one to come. They were concerned because they weren't sure if He was actually the prophet John was waiting for. "For John came neither eating nor drinking, and they say, 'He has a demon.' The Son of Man came eating and drinking, and they say, 'Look at him! A glutton and a drunkard, a friend of tax collectors and sinners!' Yet wisdom is justified by her deeds" (Matt. 11:18–19 ESV).

The people were trying to figure out why Jesus would come and spend so much time caring for people who weren't interested in the religious traditions of the day. After all, if He was *their* prophet, He should live inside *their* rules. Right?

But Jesus had a different way about Him. He looked past the fear of rejection and name-calling to care deeply for people. The people He was most interested in developing relationships with were the people He knew God cared deeply for simply because they were people. What if we had the same sense of compassion for humanity that Jesus had when He was here on earth? How would that change things in our world?

8

My Prayer in the Mosque

For I am the LORD your God who takes hold of your right hand
and says to you, Do not fear; I will help you.

Isaiah 41:13

I was working with a group in Saudi Arabia concerned with interfaith discussions. King Abdullah had invested millions of US dollars to start an interfaith center in Austria, and I was talking with a few members of the team to investigate how I might interact with them. I believe God has fashioned me to have a calm spirit when it comes to discussing issues like this, so Jamie Jo and I were trying to test if God was calling us to engage at a practical level.

We'd been working with teenagers for nearly fifteen years, and we both felt like there were incredible opportunities we could create for Muslim and Christian teenagers to learn how to talk with one another. The fear on both sides was articulated clearly, as the post-puberty mind becomes a parrot for its surroundings.

When we question faith at KIVU, our summer camp in Colorado, we have an opportunity for God's Spirit to wrap Himself around the hearts and minds of the teenagers in attendance. We don't try to tell kids what to think, but rather we try to create fertile environments so they can think. We allow them to live inside of Paul's claim, "For since the creation of the world God's invisible qualities—his eternal power and divine nature—have been clearly seen" (Rom. 1:20). I firmly believe those attributes speak a whole lot louder than any sermon given by any local pastor.

As we learned how to speak to teenagers from all backgrounds, we began to find that most teenagers think in a very similar fashion. They long to know what it's like to live in a world of honesty, they want *anyone* to reach out and care for them, and they live to know the truth.

Most evangelical teenagers today feel like they've been sold a bag of behavioral goods. Their faith communities focus on things like don't drink alcohol, don't smoke, don't have sex before marriage, read your Bible, and do your quiet times.

They don't understand what it may mean to incorporate their faith into the real world with their friends, their teachers, and their coaches. They're not being taught how to know Jesus and walk with Him every single day. And so they become increasingly disinterested in God. They see God as a parent in the sky who is watching over them to see if they are going to be able to "perform" their faith. And we wonder why they are leaving the church in droves.

The latest figures show that nearly 80 percent of teenagers who are raised in Christian homes and go off to college reject their faith by the end of their freshman year. While searching for an answer to this population decline, I've come to think:

It's not God's fault.

It's not the teenagers' fault.

It's *our* fault.

It's the parents and the leaders who have created the compartments of safety and performance that we cling to. We create environments where teenagers are supposed to succeed, but they're filled with all kinds of dos and don'ts.

As a youth leader, I've spent an enormous amount of time creating programs where teenagers can measure up spiritually. We've created so many hoops for today's teenagers to jump through, they often get lost in the maze. Show up to church, read the Bible, memorize Scripture, do this next forty-day plan step by step . . . all promising to bring them closer to God. But the two greatest commandments have nothing to do with any of that. Jesus said to love God and love others (see Matt. 22:37–40). That's it. He claimed *all* the law and the prophets hung on those two commandments.

So when I went to the Arabian Peninsula to speak of this simple way of living, there were more than a few eyebrows raised.

The Man on the Street

My first indication I was on to something interesting happened on a clear day in the large downtown area of a predominantly Muslim city. I find it exciting to see the sights in the Arabic world, smell the foods of Arabic culture, and if I can, take in a conversation over Turkish coffee. My wife and I were walking down the street, hopping in and out of the small rug boutiques, when something caught her eye. She and her friend decided they had to go to this one place across the corner while I was busy looking at some ancient Arab artifacts. No sooner had they crossed the street into the new store than I heard my name. "Mr. Braner," a man called out. "Mr. Braner!" He came running toward me.

There's no question how much I enjoy the Arabic world, but it's a little strange to be in an unfamiliar place and hear such a familiar call. I turned to see an Arab man dressed in his full-length traditional Muslim robe. He wore a red-checkered square cloth on his head, adorned with two black circular belt-like accessories. The locals call this wardrobe the thobe and ghutra.

Smiling from ear to ear, he reached for my hands and began kissing them. "Mr. Braner, I so appreciate you. I thank you so much. Thank you for coming to my country. Thank you for loving my people." I was more than a little embarrassed, not knowing exactly what this guy was talking about.

"Mister, I don't know you, but I would really like to. Would you mind joining me for a cup of coffee?"

"I would be honored."

We walked a few blocks over to his local coffee shop. He ordered for us, as my Arabic was rudimentary. And we talked. We didn't have to talk very long before I learned his name was Mr. Aziz and he was a Sunni Muslim national. He worshiped at one of the mosques we could see in the distance. He had been at one of the seminars I was doing for local international school kids, and evidently was moved by the way I cared for the Muslim faith and the teenagers in the neighborhood.

"Most Christians just come here and try to evangelize people. It comes from years of missionary work, and you know that doesn't go very far here. After all, it's illegal in my country to try to share your faith without consent from the local you speak to. You must be very careful not to offend the people you are talking to. My government takes this very seriously."

"I understand," I replied as respectfully as I could. "I'm just here to see if there's a way we can talk to one another. I realize my country is going through some real pain due to terrorism, misunderstandings, and fear about your faith. I believe we can be honest with each other. We can describe our differences and still be friends. We don't have to hate anymore."

His eyes welled up with tears. "Oh, Mr. Braner, thank you. Thank you so much for loving my country. I can see it in your eyes. I can hear it in your voice. I can sense it in your spirit. Thank you."

We talked for an hour or so before I realized my wife and her shopping mate were outside looking for me.

"Mr. Aziz, I have to excuse myself. I'm honored to call you my friend. Can I pray with you?"

I prayed for his family, for his job, and for God's Spirit to move in his life. He prayed for my time in the Gulf and asked Allah to move with me on my mission of peace.

And that was it.

There wasn't any altar call.

I didn't give him a tract to read when he got home.

We talked about Jesus for about half of our conversation, but I trust God will move in my new friend's heart at whatever pace God wants to move. I was honored to make a new friend.

The King's College

As my friendships in the region started to grow, I got a call. A friend asked if I would be interested in giving a presentation at the newly designed King Abdullah University of Science and Technology. I'd never heard of it but I thought, *Sounds like an adventure. Let's go.*

We bought tickets on Saudi Airlines to fly from the eastern part of the country to Jeddah. If you ever fly Saudi Airlines, you'll quickly see how religion plays a *huge* part in everyday life in Saudi Arabia.

We walked on the plane, and on the side of the aircraft it read, "Allah Bless You," right there on the 747. As soon as the plane began to move, there was a reading from the Quran and a prayer. I looked at my friend on the flight and whispered, "I hope that's not due to any track record for landings or anything." We laughed out loud.

And then I looked around to the people sitting in the aircraft. All the men were dressed in solid white terrycloth towels. And that's it. No Under Armour shorts protecting us from seeing parts that need not be seen.

Just a terrycloth towel for the trip to Mecca.

You see, the airplane to Jeddah is the entryway for many Muslims to start their spiritual journey to Mecca. And as one of the five pillars of Islam, it is required they journey in the simplest form, right down to the clothes they don't wear.

So here I am sitting on a plane bound for Jeddah, Saudi Arabia, with two hundred of my closest Hajj friends. *How on earth did a guy from Arkansas find his way here?* I thought.

When we arrived in Jeddah we were met by a driver from the King Abdullah University of Science and Technology

(KAUST), who escorted us an hour north along the Red Sea. Once again, the sights, the sounds, the smells, and all there was to see around me were mesmerizing. We entered the school through three levels of security and found KAUST to be one of the most magnificent universities on the planet. The architecture was world-renowned, the students were the smartest engineers in the world, and the hospitality was second to none.

We toured the campus mosque and spoke to leading university officials, and I gave my presentation on how we could begin to spark meaningful conversations between Western faith cultures and Middle Eastern cultures. It was an experience I'll never forget, as many Muslim students were weeping with joy at the prospect of eliminating the need for international ill will. They knew down deep there was a way, but they just didn't have anyone to lead them to possibilities yet.

"It's really not rocket science," I said, trying to fit into an environment I had no business being in. "Both Jesus and Muhammad talked about sacrifice. Both spoke of being able to serve one another. Both were determined to love their neighbor. So if we can start there and move into a relationship built on common bonds instead of always pointing out our differences (and there are many), God's Spirit might have an opportunity to transform our hearts to love one another." Great applause rang out over the auditorium.

My Prayer with Mr. Abdulla

Then I got the most interesting call of all. Evidently a string of connections made its way into the Saudi business community, and a businessman called me to meet. He was also interested in knowing how I was able to unite Christians and Muslims under one banner, especially when talking about young people. I took a taxi from KAUST to my new friend's business office and was escorted to the top floor. I stopped at the reception desk, and the young man working the phones said, "Mr. Abdulla will see you now, sir." He opened a door to a modest but fine business office, and Mr. Abdulla was on the other side of the desk with a huge smile on his face. "Mr. Braner, welcome to my home."

I was a bit intimidated as Mr. Abdulla has longstanding relationships with officials in Saudi Arabia and in Washington, DC. I'd seen Mr. Abdulla on a few occasions when attending Muslim/Christian meetings in America, but a one-on-one meeting was something entirely different.

"So, you are interested in Jesus?" he asked.

"Yes, sir. I've been a follower of Jesus most of my life," I responded.

"So what are you doing here in Saudi?"

"With all due respect, sir, I believe if Jesus were here on earth today, he'd probably be here talking with people in Saudi."

He looked at me quizzically through his small reading glasses, "Are you looking to convert Saudis, Mr. Braner?"

"No, sir. I believe conversion is God's job. I intend to allow God to keep His job, and maybe find some commonalities between Christianity and Islam."

"Hmm." He sounded puzzled. "What do you think about the Great Commission as it's outlined in the Bible, in Matthew, I think?" he asked.

"Well, sir. Jesus told the disciples to go and make other disciples. The word *disciple* means to learn, to teach, and to follow. So I guess I think the Great Commission is about telling people about Jesus and teaching them how He taught us to live in the world."

He laughed out loud. "You're among very few Christians I know who think this way, Mr. Braner."

I laughed through the awkwardness, not knowing exactly where he was going with this line of questioning.

"What do you think about the Trinity?" he asked.

I knew this question would be coming. It was one most Christians tripped on when speaking to Muslims. You see, Muslims believe Allah is God, and there are no others. They think Trinitarian Christians actually believe in three gods, moving our faith into the realm of the polytheist. When we say we worship God the Father, God the Son, and God the Spirit, it is heard by a Muslim as worship of three gods. But most Christians certainly wouldn't consider themselves polytheists.

"Well, Mr. Abdulla. I'm not sure how the Trinity actually works. All I know is, in the Bible, God is a Creator, Jesus calls Himself and His Father One, and Jesus claims He has to leave in order that the Spirit may come, sent by the Father in Jesus's name. I wish I had all the answers to technically work through that with you, but I'm just learning. After all, I do know you don't believe in the Trinitarian God, and until I have a good answer, I'd really like to defer that one for a later meeting."

He stopped rubbing his chin. "So you don't have an answer?"

I felt like I'd just missed the winning field goal for my high school football team.

"No, sir. I don't."

131

He smiled. "You are definitely one of my favorite Christians."
We laughed and I asked, "Why, sir?"

"Most Christians who want to talk with me about multi-faith issues come to me with arrogant attitudes. They think they know everything, and they're afraid to admit sometimes when they don't have it all wrapped up. I believe you, Mr. Braner. You don't have it figured out, and you're not trying to fit your life in the usual box. I admire that."

He looked down at his watch. "I'm sorry. You'll have to excuse me for a bit. It's my prayer time, and I never miss."

"Well, sir. If you don't mind, I'd like to join you."

"Mr. Braner, this is a Muslim tradition. It's a sacrament for my faith. I'm sure you'll be fine right here."

"Mr. Abdulla, I don't mean to be an intrusion, but if we are going to share our most intimate thoughts on faith and life, don't you think we might start by praying together?" I asked humbly.

"Have you ever prayed with a Muslim?"

"No, sir."

"I'd be delighted to show you."

And for the next fifteen minutes or so, Mr. Abdulla walked me through the traditions of praying with a Muslim. I had no idea it was such an ordeal. First, there's a practice by which every person has to wash his whole body.

Mr. Abdulla showed me I had to wash from my hands to my elbows, from my feet to my knees, my face, and my mouth.

"This represents a cleanliness before God," he shared. Then we pulled out small Arabian-style rugs and placed them on the ground. We already had our shoes off. He looked at me and said, "Just follow what I do." I nodded. "Allah Akbar . . ." he began. And for the next several minutes Mr. Abdulla showed me how to kneel, stand, prostrate myself, kneel again, stand again, and all the while he was praying in Arabic.

After it was over he looked at me. "I bet you want to know what I was saying."

"Not really," I answered quickly.

"What?" he asked.

"With all due respect, I get it. I get that you're praying to your god and asking him for wisdom, blessing, and protection. I know you want him to bless your business, your family, and ultimately lead you to a place of knowing him in a more intimate way."

He smiled. "Pretty good, Mr. Braner. What were you praying?" he asked me.

"The only thing I knew to pray. 'Our Father, Who art in heaven, hallowed be Thy name. Thy kingdom come, Thy will be done, on earth as it is in heaven.'"

And in that moment, tears welled up in my new friend's eyes. And he hugged me tight.

"We're going to be friends for a long time, my friend," he whispered in my ear.

——◆——

This is the point in the story when most of my evangelical friends think I'm absolutely crazy. "You prayed with a Muslim . . . to Allah?"

No, I didn't pray to Allah.

I prayed with my new friend who happened to be praying to Allah. I prayed the same way I always pray; it just looked a little different.

But in that sacred moment of friendship, common bond, and two grown men seeking to find God in the only way they knew how, I felt the Spirit of God with overwhelming power. There have only been a few times in my life when I can look back on my prayer times and honestly say I felt God show up, and this was one of them. For the first time in my life, I knew God was in the middle. Sure it didn't look like how my Sunday school teacher at the Baptist church in Little Rock, Arkansas, had taught me to pray, but there was something going on between Mr. Abdulla and me. A spiritual connection bridged our differences, and our common bond of friendship spoke louder than the apologetics we were trained in. For a split second, I felt like the world had a chance to spin the right direction.

We didn't have to fight. We didn't have to hate. We didn't have to argue about truth. We had the opportunity to respect one another, love one another, and serve one another, even though we both thought the other needed something more.

When I talk about no fear, this is the kind of courage it will take for the Spirit of God to dwell on earth today. We don't need another five-part series. We don't need another thirty-day challenge. We have enough information to dwell on the truth of the gospel, but in our truth we need to have the bravery to stand up to the things we most fear and look into the heart of another human, knowing we're both longing for the same hard answers in life.

When I read about the life of Jesus, I think His methods were similar. In His own declaration of the kingdom of God, He didn't fear the Samaritan woman. He didn't fear that she was living outside the principles and guidelines of the kingdom. He didn't fear the fact Samaritans worshiped in their own version of the temple. He didn't have to argue through the truth with her. He simply made Himself available to a well-known Jewish enemy He knew was searching for meaning. She'd long had the story to validate her version of God, and she was still searching for the answers that would provide living water in her life. When Jesus chose to sit with her, He knew all the ill in her world, and He began with the most basic of human needs, showing her how to drink from the fountain of life and never thirst again (see John 4:14).

The crazy things about my Muslim friends are they know about Jesus, they believe He was born of a virgin, they believe He was an anointed one who walked the earth, and they even believe in the Second Coming when He will come and reign. But for some reason, because they deny the other important parts of the Christian narrative, we alienate them and run to hide behind our brutal mountain of truth, estranging them from any discussions about worship.

In no way is this a call that we have to accept some sort of universal language that all people are going to the same place, but it is a beginning of recognizing we have some common bonds of faith and friendship we can work on.

We have the chance, through our friendships, to share why we believe Jesus is the Son of God. We have the opportunity to explore the concept of the Trinity with our Muslim neighbors. It's an amazing time in history, and we're able to share the most intimate parts of our core being with people who have a tremendous amount of a common belief system already in place.

But because of the twenty-four-hour-news-cycle media looking for another story for people to tune in to, our fear is almost continually reinforced, and we run and hide to places where our Muslim brothers and sisters can't commune with us.

After our prayer meeting, Mr. Abdulla took me to his favorite local restaurant around the corner from his office. We talked about the darkness surrounding terrorism, the ability for both our faith traditions to embrace the life and teachings of Jesus, and even of ways we might be able to continue bridging the divide by forming friendships around the world. I told him, "Well, I deal with teenagers and university students. Why don't we start there?"

And this monumental meeting led to another program we've just begun in Colorado.

9

Inviting Muslim Teenagers to My Home

Do not be afraid; you will not be put to shame. Do not fear disgrace; you will not be humiliated.

Isaiah 54:4

In 2012 I invited a group of teenagers from the Middle East to come to our summer camp in Colorado, where they could experience the way evangelical Christian summer camps operate. I truly believe their acceptance of our program was miraculous in the very least. I mean, think about it: How many Christian mothers and fathers would be willing to ship their teenagers around the world to an event driven by a faith tradition they had come to hate so much? The outcome was nothing short of miraculous as a group of Christians,

Muslims, and critics had a chance to stay in a Spirit-filled environment.

The Christian Setup

I knew from the moment I concocted this program there would be issues with Christians who were skeptical of my agenda. The first step was to help my staff understand the purpose of this cross-cultural, cross-faith epic moment.

"Here's the deal," I said. "We know what we believe. We know Jesus is the Son of God. We know there's One God who created all things and holds all things together. We know we have an abundant life promised as we hold to the teachings of Jesus. What we don't know is how our friends will respond to our basic truths. So let's have a three-pronged approach."

1. Let's be careful to translate our words of conversion.

We absolutely want our friends to follow Jesus, but the words we learned in evangelism class are often offensive to other cultures. So for the next couple of weeks, as our Muslim friends are here, let's be aggressive *listeners*.

Let's listen to their culture.

Let's roll out the red carpet of hospitality.

Let's listen to how they worship, how they pray, and how they might express their own faith traditions in an alien world.

So, instead of pulling out the "four spiritual laws" tract and guiding them down the Romans road, let's take two weeks to try something new. It doesn't mean we don't want to talk about Jesus; it may just look different for the next couple of weeks.

2. We're not Universalists.

The pendulum can swing from one side of the conversation to the other so fast that we run from the very foundational truths that brought us here. We're not embracing a soft message of the gospel as so many of my evangelical friends fear but rather we're going on a spiritual expedition of sorts. We have a duty to ask questions about the God of the Bible, so let's be sure we ask similar questions about the Allah of the Quran. It seems like all the news media stories we hear are about how violence in the Middle East comes from a core belief within Islam, so let's respectfully ask them how and why, and if they adhere to the same principles the suicide bombers use in Iraq and Afghanistan.

Be careful not to leave your foundation. We are here to live like Jesus, teach like Jesus, and employ a gospel message that is centered on His life, death, and ultimate resurrection.

3. Let's do what we do well.

Let's continue to live out the gospel in our everyday life. Let's continue our spiritual journey as our Muslim friends engage in life with us. Let's invite them to the messiness of faith so they may see, feel, and be impacted by the synergy we've worked so hard to develop. I believe if we are sensitive to our friends and find common places to exist, we'll see God show up in the middle and do *amazing* things.

The Muslim Setup

It was harder to articulate the Muslim orientation, as I'm not Arabic and haven't lived with the cultural impact of the Middle East. But as you can imagine, for many of my young Muslim friends this was their first trip out of the Middle East, and I wanted to make sure they felt the hospitality Americans can bring.

When they arrived for their time at camp, I spoke with them for an entire afternoon. I made sure they knew most Americans saw Islam as a violent faith, and that many of our American students would be skeptical about them, fearing they were terrorists. Some of our students would feel as though we had invited the enemy, so they might get questions about Allah, Muhammad, praying five times a day, and even questions about Mecca and the Hajj (the journey Muslims take on their pilgrimage).

I told them we had taken pork off the menu so they didn't have to worry about eating the turkey bacon or the turkey sausage in the morning, and they looked at me in shock.

"You would do that for us?" they asked.

"Absolutely. Whatever it takes for us to show you we can love well here as we develop relationships. I want to provide you with a safe place."

And then I helped them through evangelism.

"Look. Many of our students come from Christian homes that place a high priority on converting their friends. They believe if you die without Jesus in your heart, you're destined to spend eternity in hell. And so, if you find yourself in a conversation with an American Christian sharing these principles, just think 'They must love me a whole lot,' because they do. They may not express it well, but they really don't want any of their friends to suffer in the afterlife. Please don't be offended by that, and take it into consideration as you go through our program."

The stage was set. We were well on our way to seeing if it was even possible to unite two religions under one banner of summer adventure. I was a little nervous, hoping this wouldn't be the start of World War III. But in truth, I knew God's Spirit would guide us, and we would have the opportunity to share our lives with people from a totally different environment.

The First Day

I gave my friends a standing ovation the first day I introduced them to the two hundred other students in the auditorium. I applauded their courage to love and to take a risk, and invited them to test the program at their leisure. We got them signed up for classes, and they were as excited as any young child would be on Christmas morning. Eager to try new activities, these kids turned out to be exactly the same as their American counterparts.

They all needed to love and be loved.

They all needed to be known.

They all longed for attention.

They all needed to be valued.

I started our Christian worldview institute and made sure they knew we were going to talk through some basic apologetics and basic theologies of Jesus, but we were open to any questions they may have as we plowed through the story of the Bible.

"The Institute," as we call it, has turned out to be a safe place for students to ask intimidating questions they tend to be afraid of in their own spheres of influence. The validity of the Bible, the existence of God, and the relevance of Jesus in their daily lives make up some of the questions teenagers and college students are interested in. So as a teacher, facilitator, and dreamer, I have the opportunity to guide those discussions, even when my Muslim friends are sitting in the front row.

Each night I went to the leaders to make sure we were talking the same language. I wanted to make sure we didn't offend and provided an opportunity to discover our differences in real time. Each night I was amazed to find the Muslim leaders more excited than the day before.

On one particular day, I decided to do a section on Christology, mainly from Colossians 1. I talked about Jesus being the image of the invisible God, the firstborn over all creation, and the One in whom all things hold together. At the end of the session one of the more vocal Muslim leaders came to me and said, "I think we need to talk."

And in an instant, I was afraid. What had I said? What had I done? Had I reached a point of difference so far there was no way to return?

I decided to take my new friend out to dinner to make sure we could share a meal through our differences. We drove to my favorite restaurant in Durango, Colorado, and I sat across the table and asked, "So what did you need to ask me?"

He looked at me as a man intently ready to tear down all the walls of faith I built up and asked, "So . . . why are all Christians Republicans?"

I laughed out loud.

How in the world did my friend draw such a conclusion?

We had made it a clear point to distance all of our discussions from politics. But he was interested in the connection between politics and faith that was so prominent in the American political system. It was absolutely *amazing*!

For the next two hours we talked about how issues like abortion and gay marriage drove the political discussions in America. We talked about how there was a new breed of politicians rising, and were able to have these discussions in a public space. We talked about the need for more connection between America and the Middle East, for more connection between Christians and Muslims, and ultimately for more people who are willing to take the call of Jesus seriously in their lives.

———

You see, I've become a man *not afraid*. I believe the power of the gospel is in the man Jesus. We may spend a great amount of time working over the processes by which God works on the planet today, but if we just boil it all down to a few simple steps, it's amazing to watch God work.

At the end of our time at the KIVU program, the Muslim leaders stood on stage in front of the whole KIVU student body, and one of them declared, "I've heard a lot about American Christianity, and even more about America's view of Jesus. But I've never seen Jesus until I met you all here at this place. Thank you for showing us who Jesus is. We have a lot to talk about going home."

Can you believe that? My naysayer friends always ask, "So, did they convert?" To which I always respond, "I don't know."

It's not my job to convert people.

It's not my job to sell God.

It's not my job to manipulate people through a program or through worship so they make a decision based on emotion.

It's not my job to outthink someone to the cross.

But it is my job to put aside the fear in my life of living as Jesus asked me to live, and do just that. When I do, God's Spirit begins to work on the hearts and minds of my friends I engage with, and *crazy stuff* happens.

To date, we've seen hundreds of Muslim teens at our camp in Colorado and abroad. We've had incredible reactions to people seeking, searching, and exploring the life and times of Jesus. And we will continue. Sometimes it looks like a traditional Bible study full of eager students wanting to know what the Bible says. And sometimes it takes the form of sharing a meal and learning about Muslim traditions.

We need not fear the unknown. After all, "the one who is in you is greater than the one who is in the world" (1 John 4:4). And I know our battle isn't against flesh and blood; it's against principalities we cannot see. It's against the evil in the world that draws all men and women away from God. So when I put on the armor of God to go out in the world, what do I have to be afraid of?

I had a coach who, one time, challenged me with the question, "What is the worst possible thing that could happen to you right now?"

"I guess I could die, coach," I responded.

"Well, that wouldn't be that bad, would it? I mean, you would go off to heaven, right?"

And I stood in silence.

If the worst thing you can think about in forming a relationship with someone you fear is that they turn on you and kill you, how bad is that, *really*? So the worst thing that could happen to me is that I go and see God?

I'll take it.

Fear has the ability to keep us from exploring the possibilities of our neighbors around the world coming to join our adventure. Fear has the ability to make us live inside the shadows of safety. Fear has the ability to paralyze our thoughts and actions to the point of irrelevance.

From one adventurer to another, don't be afraid. God didn't give you that spirit, and you're giving in to the enemy. Don't be afraid. Don't be scared. What you have is more precious than silver or gold, namely a God who loves you and cares for you enough to sacrifice His own Son, Jesus Christ, to reconcile you to Himself.

The most compelling adventures are those that happen when we recognize fear, address it, and move to a place of reliance on what God is doing in the hearts and minds of others.

We don't need to come up with a new formula.

We don't have to systematize God.

Just stand in the core of who you are and allow God to do the rest.

What an exciting life we get to live!

OVERCOMING FEAR OF
Culture

10

Christians, Abortion, and Fear

Do not be afraid of those who kill the body but cannot kill the soul. Rather, be afraid of the One who can destroy both soul and body in hell.

Matthew 10:28

Working with students always brings with it an amazing sense of contributing to the growth and foundation of a new generation. This feeling is only offset when you see young people make poor decisions and bad choices that are avoidable.

Each year I spend a fair amount of time helping students see the value of marriage in the context of their own sexuality. We talk about the purpose of sex and the reason it's best kept within the confines of marriage, and we talk at length about how to succeed in relationships today. But boy, is it difficult.

With the world screaming at them in an oversexualized way, it's no wonder so many students struggle to remain pure until they're married. From television to film to music to magazines, kids are inundated with sexual messages. The confusion they're working through often seems like an endless uphill battle for those of us engaged in a boots-on-the-ground operational role.

Not long ago, I got the dreaded phone call from one of my students, who confessed she was pregnant. She and a strong Christian guy were in a dedicated relationship, but in a moment of weakness they had become sexually active, and they ended up in a predicament. They had been having sex for nearly three months and had kept it a secret from their parents, friends, and mentors. They thought they could manage their relationship but now were staring pregnancy in the face.

"I know getting an abortion is wrong, but I'm not ready to care for a baby," she said.

This brings us to the greatest fear reaction of our tribe, one that is nothing short of toxic. Since the Roe v. Wade decision of 1973, the faith community has tried to figure out how we can stand up for the lives of the unborn. A "righteous" anger resides in the pro-life tribe, and the same anger is evident among pro-choice people.

In my line of work, I don't want any young women to have to deal with such trauma without proper channels to help. No well-meaning human being in their right mind can think a teenager is ready to be a parent. But we also have a high regard for human life. And there the issue begins to present itself as a paradox, quickly taking ugly sides.

"Well, she shouldn't be having sex if she's not ready to be pregnant." I can hear the whispers from my pro-life colleagues.

"This is why abortion is legal, to protect teenagers who make mistakes from unwanted pregnancies," I hear from another corner.

So what are we to do?

We've heard countless sermons helping us understand how God is the giver of life. We've seen research dedicated to proving life begins at conception. We've been a part of protests. We've elected officials. We've even tried to implement laws whereby an expectant mother would have to go through training to fully understand the consequences of an abortion.

For decades now, we've tried to halt this incredibly awful practice, with no real win in sight. The number of abortions continues to climb, even though many of us calculate our voting behavior to include the variables of pro-life candidates. So what's the deal?

If we've given all our known methodologies to answer the problem, and we haven't been able to see the solution, what's actually happening?

I believe we're scared. I believe fear has invaded our hearts so much that we are paralyzed and unable look at potential different options.

Abortion became a national political conversation when it entered the legal arena. We've been trained to think of abortion through the lens of politicians, laws, and judgments. Some have even maneuvered the conversation to women's health. But what is the Jesus-following person to do with legal matters? After all, didn't Jesus say, "Give to Caesar what is Caesar's and give to God what is God's"?

What if we had the opportunity to lay our fear aside and really begin to attack this situation from another vantage point? It would almost be like seeing the known rules as a game and reinventing how we play it. This is where fear meets real-world scenarios that we're called to help handle as people who love God and love others.

Solutions Discovered in the Most Unlikely Places

Not long ago, I created a silly game called Braner Ball. Yes, it's named after me because I invented it, and each time I introduce the game to a new group of students I use the tagline, "The best game ever invented."

The rules for the game are simple.

We meet at home plate on a baseball field with six different items to be distributed into the field.

We have a football, a baseball, a soccer ball, a whiffle ball, a volleyball, and a Frisbee.

When a batter gets up to start the game, their first action is to distribute the items to the outfield. A Braner Ball batter can throw, kick, knee, or do whatever they feel is necessary to get all the items into the outfield. But here's the catch: once the first item goes out to the outfield, the defense has to remain in their positions until the final ball is placed. They can't move. Then, when the final ball is distributed to the outfield, the defense must strategically get all the items back to home plate inside a plastic trash can for an out.

In the meantime, the base runner has to go all the way around the bases to score a run.

There are no singles, doubles, or triples, just a homerun or nothing. The only way to get that runner out is to fill the plastic trash can with all six items. Those are the only rules I share with the teams. It's up to them to figure out whatever strategy works best.

Some try to assign the kicked balls to different players.

Some try to run the balls in while others throw them to a cut-off player.

But overall, it's pretty simple. Get items into the outfield, and then try to get them in to home plate before the runner scores.

Every now and then, I'll get a question from the opposing team: "Can we move the trash can?" And then the fun begins. All of a sudden the rules they heard have become guidelines, and the rules of baseball start to gray.

I've had students kick the balls from second base while the defense has to remain in position. I've had some carry the trash can with them on their trek around the bases.

I've even had some try and hide the balls so the other team can't get them until it's too late. Cries from the other team emerge. "That's cheating!"

To which I ask, "Why?"

"They can't carry the trash can!" they shout.

"Why not? It wasn't in the rules," I'll answer.

You see, one of the most important object lessons in Braner Ball is to see and recognize the power of preconceived ideas as the students enter the game seeing the baseball field.

They think the only way to win is to participate in the rules of baseball, softball, kickball, or whatever game they've previously played on the ball diamond. But what if the rules could be changed?

What if the arena they played in looked like a baseball field but actually became something entirely different?

This is what I'm suggesting in our lives as believers when we participate in conversations that become "toxic," such as the abortion debate. What if the arena changed? Instead of seeing abortion as a legal problem that can only be solved by legal means, what if we changed the game?

What if we started addressing the real needs of the teenage mothers and tried to meet them in their space of fear, pain, and rejection? Some may scream, "But you can't do it like that!" To which I would reply, "Why not? What we're doing now isn't working, so let's try something new."

What if we began thinking about abortion differently?

A Talk with the Good Doctor

I have a close friend who's an OB/GYN in a local hospital. She is a dedicated follower of Jesus and finds herself in a pinch when a woman comes to her asking her to terminate a pregnancy.

She prays with her patients. She tries to sway them to keep the baby. She talks of adoption and other methods to ensure she is keeping with her view of the sanctity of life. She sits on her city council. She lobbies Congress for aggressive abortion laws.

But in the end, she says the number of abortions remains about the same.

So what happened when the good doctor decided to change the rules?

Just the other day she and I had an intense conversation about how to share her faith with patients without crossing any legal lines. We tried to brainstorm how we might present the abortion debate to a pregnant mother in a way that may sway her to protect the life growing inside her.

"With the invention of the new 3D MRIs we can now show mothers the baby growing right inside their uterus. It's amazing! The results are astonishing," she said. "For every ten mothers who come in for an abortion, after seeing the MRI nine decide to keep the baby and figure out how best to approach adoption or foster care."

And the game starts to change.

If 90 percent of women who initially wanted to terminate a pregnancy see this MRI, why are we spending so much money lobbying Congress? We know the approval rating of the current congressional class is lower than 15 percent, so why are we addicted to changing the law?

We're so blinded by the idea that someone is either pro-life or pro-choice, we're unable to even engage in new strategies to change the hearts of young mothers.

And every election cycle, politicians try to drum up the fear debate of who is pro-life and who is pro-choice, as if they are someone who can actually do something to change the game. The arena needs to change, because the people who promise to actually do something about the issue seem to get in office and become disinterested in actually solving something. Instead of looking for a legal answer to the problem, maybe we have to rethink the arena we play in to solve the real problem.

Caring for People, Not Power

It really means we have to go back to a fundamental "care for our fellow humans" approach.

We don't want to fight abortion; we want to fight for the life of a fellow human. We don't want to demonize people who feel like abortion is their only way to survive; we want to give people viable options that will care for them and the unborn. And sometimes that might mean taking an unusual step toward the most fear-filled environment.

I have a longtime friend who stands up for the unborn. He doesn't care who gets the credit for success; he simply wants to see the number of abortions reduced in this country until we find another way to support our precious teenagers.

He decided it was high time to put the fear behind him, lay down the posters of dead babies, and stop shouting at innocent passersby who didn't understand the reason for the protests around the Planned Parenthood complex. He decided to set up a meeting with the managing director of Planned Parenthood. I can hear it now from my evangelical friends: "He's meeting with the devil?"

My friend thought it would be more important to approach the problem head-on instead of trying to seize power from an institution that provides women's healthcare to some of the most vulnerable in our society.

They met over lunch on a Wednesday afternoon, and my friend outlined the agenda: (1) He cared deeply for the women who were coming to Planned Parenthood for an abortion. (2) He cared deeply for the life of the unborn children who didn't have a say in the procedure. (3) He communicated the high value he thought Planned Parenthood brought to the community through education, training, and cancer screenings.

Many thought it was outlandish for him to try to meet with "the enemy." But my buddy was sure that, if given the chance, he could outline the things they found in common and they might have a chance to come to an agreement to begin a dialogue to reach both of their goals. Because, let's be honest, no human being wants to rip apart the body of another human being for the sake and safety of their own selfish future dreams. Or do they?

It was amazing to hear the tale of this meeting and my friend's risk. He told me how he and the director both shared a common desire to advocate for the health and safety of the young women who came in the clinic. Both of them wanted to reduce the number of abortions in their community, but admittedly there were pressures from others who maintained the Planned Parenthood track record on abortion.

They ended the meeting agreeing to explore options where they could reach out to their community in three ways:

1. Education. Most parents and young people receive their education about sexuality through the media. They have no real idea how to cope with the emotional, physical, and mental effects an active sex life has for teens.

2. Healthcare. Both were concerned about adequate healthcare in the region. They both wanted the best-in-class women's healthcare for their patients.

3. Advocacy. Both came to the end of their conversation wanting to promote healthier sexual activity. My friend wanted to help young men and women see how special sexuality can be in the confines of a monogamous relationship, and his Planned Parenthood counterpart wanted to see the STD rate in the region lowered. They

may have seen the morality of sexuality a bit differently, but their desired outcome was similar.

None of this could have happened if my friend had decided to dig his heels in and hide behind the shadows of "they are my enemy." He had to take a risk. He felt it necessary to have a conversation with his assumed adversary that was productive instead of damaging to the cause.

We need more people who are following Jesus to be willing to risk their reputations in order to come to a resolution. If the goal is to reduce the number of abortions, we need to steer clear of the power mongering going on at all levels of politics, in or out of the church.

Oh, and by the way, the girl who called me for advice on getting an abortion? My wife and I had a chance to walk her through the pregnancy step-by-step, counseling her through the various stages. We supported her and her family as they found the news to be less than welcome in their home church. We helped them find a place where they felt comfortable putting the baby into the arms of a loving, welcoming couple who had been waiting for a chance to be parents.

These issues aren't impossible. They do take a bit more thought and action than we usually see. They take time. They take a heart of caring for another human being, a heart that is at the core of our faith tradition.

If we're really interested in seeing the number of abortions reduced in this country, reaching out and caring for the most vulnerable must be at the top of our priority list. We don't need to be so consumed about the politicians' stump speeches but rather we need to care deeply for the teenage parents who are scared out of their minds. We need to provide shelter—physically, emotionally, and spiritually. And in the end, we remember our greatest job is to love God and love others. After all, "All the Law and the Prophets hang on these two commandments," as Jesus said (Matt. 22:40).

11

Fear of the "Other"

The Spirit you received does not make you slaves, so that you live in fear again; rather, the Spirit you received brought about your adoption to sonship. And by him we cry, "Abba, Father."

Romans 8:15

The fear that isolates people from one another is one of my greatest concerns. More specifically, the conversation in the media concerning human rights of the homosexual community poses a great threat to those who are holding tight to the past instead of looking to the future of who the modern church could be as a loving group of people that reaches out to love others. Both sides have shown such disdain for the other, and some Christian fellowships are even disbanding over their corporate stances.

Some churches believe homosexuals are no different than anyone else and have the right to marry, participate, and lead in the traditional church model. Others are taking a firm stance on homosexuality being defined as sin, leaving a whole group of people standing on the outside of the church wondering what their role can be in following Jesus. So what happens when two differing worldviews collide with one another around something as controversial as the homosexual agenda?

I realize even tackling this issue sets me up for ill will from 50 percent of my audience. But instead of providing clear-cut answers, I'd like to take a second and look at both sides in order to have a clear picture of what's really going on.

The Traditional View

Growing up in the South created in me a significantly strong stance toward the homosexual community. I can remember several classes where I was taught that the greatest evil in the world was the homosexual agenda, which was trying to reshape the Judeo-Christian moral code America was founded on. I remember friends who would say things like, "God created Adam and Eve, not Adam and Steve" to create a bedrock argument for God's creation of marriage as being between one man and one woman. And fear took root.

The New Testament Scripture used most often in defense of traditional marriage comes from 1 Corinthians 6:9–10:

> Or do you not know that wrongdoers will not inherit the kingdom of God? Do not be deceived: Neither the sexually immoral nor idolaters nor adulterers nor men who have sex with men nor thieves nor the greedy nor drunkards nor slanderers nor swindlers will inherit the kingdom of God.

Much of the tradition surrounding this verse comes from an innate hatred for sin. Those of us who are followers of Jesus are very concerned with our own struggle for a pure life; as Jesus says, "Blessed are the pure in heart, for they will see God" (Matt. 5:8). I can even hear my traditional Sunday school teachers in my memories: "See, it's plain as black and white. God doesn't bless homosexuals. They are sinners."

It is within our tradition that, as we develop deep, spiritually formative relationships, sin becomes something forgiven and forgotten, and the pursuit of righteousness is at the forefront of our existence. But somewhere between "God loves you" and the threat of some homosexual sin in the church, a space of "us versus them" is created.

Remember, I graduated from a small Christian high school that taught the same morals and values found in most conservative evangelical circles. I'd never met anyone who was gay, and the conservative teachings from my school and the teachings of my local church were all matter of fact: people who followed Jesus had some kind of divine obligation to make sure we didn't associate with people who were gay.

When I arrived at a Christian university, I was more than surprised by the number of people who claimed to be gay or were associated with the gay community. It's safe to say, I was shocked! I was a theater major, so the population percentages walking the halls with me were a little skewed, but being raised in a small town, I was far from ready to face this new normal. I experienced an interesting evolution from fear to knowing how to approach someone who believed in a different lifestyle.

The New Normal

Based on news reports concerning things like the Defense of Marriage Act and the legalization of gay marriage in many states in America, Christians have been forced to either be quiet or stand up and let their voices be heard. Many have framed the debate as a civil rights issue. And how can you argue?

For the last two hundred years many people have been hiding their sexual orientation for fear of losing their jobs and being seen as outcasts, and really haven't had a place to be vocal in the public square. Remember, only a couple of decades ago homosexuality was still something to be whispered about in the dark hallways of seedy places. To date, all tax legislation has been on the side of traditional marriage, and same-sex couples who have endured the discrimination that prevents them from receiving the rights heterosexual married couples receive have to live in the fear of someday dealing with their partner's death from arms length. The debate has also been framed as equal to a racial divide, much like the civil rights movement of the '60s and '70s, and "Freedom!" is the cry from the New Normal.

After making friends with people who chose to live an alternative lifestyle, I found my own interpretation of the Bible being scrutinized. I felt guilty claiming that gay marriage was an abomination because I had friends who were living with their partners—and they were normal humans.

They ate like I ate.

They feared like I feared.

They dreamed like I dreamed.

And I started wondering, *How can I take such a hard stance with my friends, who are all real people?*

The Tide Has Shifted

When I began my work talking with university students primarily from faith backgrounds, the message was easy. Ten years ago most Christians agreed homosexuality was something we needed to guard against. I didn't know anyone standing up for heterosexual rights or making flags symbolizing sexual freedom for men and women. It was an easy argument to make.

But in the summer of 2013 I noticed a distinct change in the rhetoric. When I began the conversation by simply asking the question, "Should we support gay marriage or fight for the rights of traditional marriage?" the overall feeling in the room was different.

For the first time in my teaching history, I noticed a barrage of students who were in support of gay marriage and were willing to argue for the rights of their friends and family members who felt comfortable enough to come out of the closet.

I even began noticing a distinct change in the numbers of adolescent teenagers who were struggling with their own sexual identity. At fifteen, sixteen, and seventeen, it seemed like there was an all-out assault to make sure they weren't gay or to make sure they could find a place accepting enough for them to express their natural tendencies. So we began a new conversation: Is gay marriage a viable option for those of us who see the world in a different way?

The easy answer is no. The tradition most of us come from would say, "The Bible says it, I believe it, so there." But could it be in the realm of possibility that the church has a duty and responsibility to examine this issue on a deeper level?

After talking with my gay friends, I have learned that for them the idea of marriage is a symbol of equality. They aren't satisfied with simply receiving civil rights as might be articulated in some sort of legislation in the civil union arena. They long for the word *marriage*, as it symbolizes a place where they can be identified as people.

Of course, my evangelical friends stand firm on the teaching of the Bible. If God condemns homosexual behavior, there's no way in the world they would ever stand for something that may lead to God's judgment in their own communities or their country at large.

For my gay friends, acknowledgment is key to acceptance. And it's not as though they are asking for acceptance of their behavior but rather they just want to be accepted as people. For my evangelical friends, the issue is the sanctity of an institution they are trying to protect. If God uses the metaphor of a bride and a bridegroom to identify His relationship with humanity, then when we water down the meaning of the word *marriage* we are negotiating with something sacred God has given.

My gay friends believe they were born that way. They believe deep down in their soul that their very DNA is fashioned to cause same-sex attraction. For my evangelical friends, they hold to the "you can manage your sin" mantra. If you don't want to do something, then you don't have to. And for the homosexual community trying to live inside the framework of a biblical lifestyle, then even if gay people have a DNA strain leading them to sin, they should be able to live a life of abstinence and deny the urge to be who they are.

My gay friends want rights. My evangelical friends look toward a place where homosexuality can be healed.

My gay friends long to be in a community. My evangelical friends want the gay community to be treated like the leper colonies of the Old Testament.

So what should we do?

How can we live within a tribe of humans with two very diametrically opposed ways of looking at the basics of human sexuality?

The Chick-fil-A Saga

In 2012 Dan Cathy, an executive and family founder of Chick-fil-A, went on radio to say, "I think we are inviting God's judgment on our nation when we shake our fist at Him and say, 'We know better than you as to what constitutes a marriage' . . . I pray God's mercy on our generation that has such a prideful, arrogant attitude to think that we have the audacity to define what marriage is about."[1] Cathy went on in a *Baptist Press* article posted a few days later that he is "guilty as charged" and is very "supportive of the family—the biblical definition of the family unit."[2]

These comments spurred a national conversation concerning the role of business in the civil rights arena. Cries from all over America filled the conversation with statements that Chick-fil-A was a company that supported the rights of traditional marriage at the expense of the homosexual community.

1. Myles Collier, "Chick-fil-A President Says 'God's Judgment' Coming Because of Same-Sex Marriage," *The Christian Post*, July 18, 2012, http://www.christianpost.com/news/chick-fil-a-president-says gods-judgment-coming-because-of-same-sex-marriage-78485/.
2. K. Allan Blume, "'Guilty as Charged,' Cathy Says of Chick-fil-A's Stand on Biblical & Family Values," *Baptist Press*, July 16, 2012, http://www.bpnews.net/BPnews.asp?ID=38271.

The news media pounced. Mr. Cathy was called everything short of a bigot. Former Arkansas governor and FOX News host Mike Huckabee called for a "Chick-fil-A Appreciation Day," and thousands lined up to buy their chicken sandwich in support of Cathy's statements. I happened to be teaching a seminar on ethics for teenagers during this time, and I asked my students what they thought.

"Imagine for a moment you come from a homosexual tradition. You hear that Chick-fil-A Appreciation Day is on Wednesday this week. When you drive by the local restaurant chain in your town, there are cars lined up around the block. What do you think about those people?" I asked.

One student raised her hand. "I guess I would feel like the community hates me for being who I am."

"But was that their intent?"

"Obviously the people who are lining up aren't in line to say they hate homosexuals. They are in line to show their support of heterosexual union."

"Yes, but what is the perception? Remember, no matter what our intent, perception dictates the reality for those who feel disenfranchised."

All of a sudden, out of nowhere, a young girl raised her hand and said, "I have a solution. What if we support heterosexual unions by waiting in line and joining the movement as a group who believes one man and one woman is the right way to define marriage?"

I didn't really see where she was going, and I was fearful her age was going to trump any epiphany we were about to have, when all of a sudden she added, "And then we set up a tent on the other side of the street and have a sign that says 'Free Chicken Sandwiches for Gay Couples.'"

I was astonished. *Why didn't I think of that?* I thought. From the mouths of babes, in one fell swoop we had a solution on the table that actually allowed for someone to express their moral conviction and then serve those whom they disagreed with.

I know the metaphor breaks down, but how many of us are so afraid of engaging in the conversation that we're blinded to our real calling, which is mainly to be servant leaders?

I watched the conversation begin to take shape nationally. I watched evangelicals who showed how much they disagreed with the homosexual agenda. But it wasn't until I read an article in the *Huffington Post* that my perception changed. The article was written by a gay man, Shane Windmeyer, who had also watched the Chick-fil-A conversation from afar. As a lifelong activist for the gay agenda and the executive director of Campus Pride, Mr. Windmeyer was more than skeptical of Mr. Cathy's comments concerning traditional marriage. So you can imagine the story when the bastion of traditional marriage decided to reach out to one of the world's most vocal gay rights advocates and just ask questions. Mr. Windmeyer reports in his article about how he was taken aback as Mr. Cathy expressed, with deep sincerity, his desire to know more about how his organization worked, what their concerns were, and how he could speak from a more educated point of view. [3]

As I read the article, I felt the tears welling up inside. In that moment I watched someone from a Jesus perspective

3. Shane L. Windmeyer, "Dan and Me: My Coming Out as a Friend of Dan Cathy and Chick-fil-A," *Huffington Post*, January 28, 2013, http://www.huffing tonpost.com/shane-l-windmeyer/dan-cathy-chick-fil-a_b_2564379.html.

reach out to someone who thought totally differently, simply in the spirit of friendship and understanding.

Mr. Cathy still believes strongly in the traditional marriage viewpoint. Mr. Windmeyer still advocates for gay marriage. But what's different about these two men who are interested in helping the world be a better place is that they were willing to see each other as human beings. They laid aside the fear of being right or wrong for the greater good of achieving an understanding of how the other lives. Each had to take some time out and listen to the other side without their personal judgment clouding their view.

The H Factor

That's the real point of the gay marriage conversation. There are people who believe strongly on both sides of the issue, but how can we come to a place where we see each other as people and stop demonizing the *other*?

The evangelical community is afraid that homosexuals are going to recruit their kids. Homosexuals are afraid evangelicals hate them and are going to subject them to hate crimes.

Evangelicals want to be the pillars of right in the community. Homosexuals don't care about the evangelical view of right and wrong.

Evangelicals see a God-given sacrament in marriage. Homosexuals see loving someone as spanning beyond traditional gender.

And both have a voice in the conversation.

We need not fear each other. There's no need to protest with long lines outside of restaurants to show the world how much you stand against a particular idea. There's no need to raise the banners of "God Hates F—s" to protest a country that's willing to have a debate.

Yes, these are important core values we are talking about.

Yes, there is a place where civil rights and biblical morality are going to clash.

But we need not fear the *discussion*.

The most intimate part of the human condition is the fear of rejection.

The foundation of the gospel is reconciliation and togetherness.

The fact God was willing to reconcile to Himself the whole of humanity and *all* the protagonist characters in the Bible searching for validation helps us understand the need *all* humankind has to connect to God.

Our homosexual friends need community and certain levels of human validation as much as we do. It doesn't mean you have to agree with the way they view life. In fact, when worldviews clash and people are willing to fight through the disagreement to search for friendship, I believe the gospel is seen clearly.

For it was Jesus who came to the earth, foregoing the accolades of heaven to live like us, to experience humanity, and to dwell *with* us on earth. Surely He saw the sins of humankind as repugnant to the host of heaven, yet He saw fit to dwell together to provide us with a relationship with God. It doesn't mean Jesus ever sacrificed His duty to purity and to providing a moral compass for humanity to follow. I won't propose that relationship equals acceptance of all behavior, but I would ask that we put our fear of the unknown aside and learn how to dwell together.

12

Fear in a "New Normal"

Be on your guard; stand firm in the faith; be courageous; be strong.

1 Corinthians 16:13

The world is trying to figure out what immigration looks like in an era of globalization. It seems like companies are more than willing to export manufacturing jobs overseas for the obvious benefit to their bottom line but aren't willing to allow those who make the goods to cross the border. Immigration in the United States has been blamed for higher crime statistics, lower wages for entry-level jobs, and being a drag on the healthcare system. But we're not the only country in this situation. A few years ago, I had a chance to present a training seminar in Amman, Jordan. I was invited to be a part of an initiative looking to bridge the ideologies of East and West. After my seminar, my host asked if I'd like to take a tour of the city, and I was more than honored to see it through the eyes of a native Jordanian.

"How is Jordan handling the aftermath of America's war in Iraq and Afghanistan?" I asked quizzically, knowing most Arabs have political opinions that spur on fun conversation.

"The hardest part of the war in the region is the fact we now have one million Iraqi refugees. After the Lebanon-Israel war we had one million Palestinian refugees, and as soon as the fighting started in Syria we also had nearly one million Syrian refugees. Each one of those provided a lower wage for jobs, so our unemployment rate here is close to 45 percent."

I sat with wide eyes as I listened to the story articulated by my business-minded friend. After all, to keep a business running the bottom line is the bottom line is the bottom line, but my friend is also a man of faith.

"So how do you deal with this problem?" I asked, trying to equate the similar problem in America. "We have nearly twelve million undocumented workers in America and most of us don't know what to do. One side says, 'They broke the law and they need to pay for it,' while the other side says, 'They came for a reason and they are fulfilling a need in America.'" I found myself trying to explain a difficult problem in America, and eventually our discussion led to faith and people.

"I believe God created all men, and we have an obligation to serve all men. If someone comes to Jordan for safety and security, I think we have a duty to reach out and help them. That's what we do when we say God loves us and our neighbors," he replied. The beauty of seeing immigration issues through the eyes of another nation is the clarity it brings to the problem.

I have friends in Arizona, Florida, Texas, and California who want to build a fence across the southern border of America because they feel the ills of illegal immigration. I have friends in the Midwest who hire illegal workers because they believe in free market capitalism. They believe if you can get labor cheap that's a part of letting the market decide how much something is worth. It's amazing how many people are afraid of the immigration topic, and you'd be surprised why.

The Danger of Violence

For some reason, Americans have a predisposition for wondering how immigrants will affect their way of living. They fear illegals, as they are seen as responsible for an increasing rate of violent crime in the last few years. Take the controversial legislation presented in 2010 to the voters in Arizona. The lobbyists for the law argued that violent crime had to be deterred and it was necessary to institute more rigorous legislation to make sure they protected the legal citizens of Arizona. But after a little research, I found,

> According to FBI statistics, violent crimes reported in Arizona dropped by nearly 1,500 reported incidents between 2005 and 2008. Reported property crimes also fell, from about 287,000 reported incidents to 279,000 in the same period. These decreases are accentuated by the fact that Arizona's population grew by 600,000 between 2005 and 2008.[1]

1. Mariano Castillo, "Crime Stats Test Rationale behind Arizona Immigration Law," *CNN Justice* (April 29, 2010), http://www.cnn.com/2010/CRIME/04/29/arizona.immigration.crime/.

The crime rate was already on the decline when the bill was introduced to the Arizona legislators. So what is the real reason the bill was introduced? Could it be crime? Or could it be the fact that we just don't like to watch our cities change color? I'm not about to accuse the Arizona legislators of being racist, but I am willing to take a long look at the reason why most of us just don't like to see our neighborhoods change their demographic. Deep in the heart of our entire psyche is the need to be a part of a tribe that represents safety, protection, and a way of life we are used to. If we are faced with the possibility of change, it makes us act in strange ways.

According to the US Census Bureau statistics in 2007, 45 percent of all births in Arizona were Hispanic. Non-Hispanic white births accounted for only 40 percent. The projection in 2007 was that by 2015 a natural minority-majority transition was going to take place and the majority of Arizona's population of six million people would be of Hispanic or Latino origin. I wonder how much legislation was due to the fact non-Hispanics were afraid they were losing.

There's no getting around the illegal human trafficking that happens in Arizona. There are certainly bad things happening when people cross the border and enter drop houses, including the use of the innocent in the sex trafficking trade. There have been countless reports of child labor laws being violated, and the general burden on schools and hospitals due to the influx of illegals is a real problem. But violence? I think not.

We are afraid of losing what we know to be normal. We don't want to have to think about dealing with the changes a new population would bring into our backyard. But is this truly the position and the heart of God, or are we allowing fear to control us?

Finding Grace in an Unlikely Place

I had a chance to visit a wonderful ministry in the heart of Phoenix. I won't mention the name because they are constantly trying to help people as *people*, often in the face of extreme opposition from Christian groups. Those who see the world in black and white can't seem to bring themselves to see people as people. More often, they see there has been a violation of law that needs to be rectified.

On a bright, sunny Thursday afternoon, I had the chance to see people who have given their lives to helping legal and illegal immigrants understand how to live in America. They try to help them develop a strong sense of the importance of education. There are doctors to provide healthcare for women and children, and there's even a place where men can learn a trade valuable to the American economy.

I stopped by a home in a predominately Hispanic neighborhood and had a chance to talk with a woman who came to America seeking a better life. We spoke through a translator so we could make sure we both understood the whole conversation.

"How did you feel when you came to America? Why did you come?" I asked this sixty-seven-year-old grandmother who had lived in America for nearly twenty years.

"I thought when I came to America I would be able to find opportunity to help my family at home. All the stories I heard were of America's welcoming of people like me," she said.

"So, how did you get here?"

"I found a company that promised to smuggle me and my family across the border so we could enter the United States. I had been trying to get a visa to come to America for years, but this man promised he would get us here and connect us with people who would provide opportunity for people like me. He didn't mention anything about documents, proper channels, or what might be waiting in terms of the immigration police."

"But now you have several children and grandchildren who are American citizens?"

"My daughter was pregnant when we arrived. When she was starting to have contractions, I was unsure how it might go, so we went to a local hospital. The doctors and nurses were so kind, and my grandson was born here in America. He has access to full American citizenship."

"But you and your daughter?"

"We are happy to provide my grandson with opportunity, but we know any time we might get a knock on the door and have to leave this country without him. Or I guess we could take him, and he could return when he's older since he's a citizen. But we live in constant fear of being found, and we have nowhere to go to get answers."

The more I talked with this woman, the more I saw in her eyes a place of sacrifice most of us have no idea exists. We don't know what it's like to live in fear we may be deported away from our loved ones. We have no idea what it means to wonder how we're going to get a job to feed our families, provide healthcare, or even get our kids an education. I realize there's a moral obligation to uphold the laws of the land, but what are we to do with the millions of stories just like this one? Do we just round up all those who've been a part of the American economy and ship them home?

The beauty of the organization I had a chance to tour is how they feel it's their responsibility to simply love people and take care of them the best they know how. They feed families, minister to their needs, and make sure they navigate within the boundaries of American law to get the attention they need to survive. It seems to me, as the church enters the discussion of immigration, we must be a people who give to "the least of these" as Jesus commanded. Remember when Jesus was talking with His disciples about the coming of the end of the age?

> Then the King will say to those on his right, "Come, you who are blessed by my Father; take your inheritance, the kingdom prepared for you since the creation of the world. For I was hungry and you gave me something to eat, I was thirsty and you gave me something to drink, I was a stranger and you invited me in, I needed clothes and you clothed me, I was sick and you looked after me, I was in prison and you came to visit me."
>
> Then the righteous will answer him, "Lord, when did we see you hungry and feed you, or thirsty and give you something to drink? When did we see you a stranger and invite you in, or needing clothes and clothe you? When did we see you sick or in prison and go to visit you?"
>
> The King will reply, "Truly I tell you, whatever you did for one of the least of these brothers and sisters of mine, you did for me." (Matt. 25:34–40)

The most beautiful part of grace is when we have a chance to extend it to those who we think don't deserve it. After all, God extended His grace of life, and life more abundantly, and by all accounts we didn't deserve it. So why are we so afraid of facing the conversation about helping illegals? Are we afraid we might be nullifying American law? Are we scared our neighborhoods might look different in the next decade?

Or are we so caught up in politics that we give way to our team rather than give to those in need?

The Truth about Immigrants in a New World

It's crazy to think how fast our world has changed in the last two decades. The digital revolution brought communication to the same speed as the microwave in our kitchen. Just as fast as we can heat leftovers for an evening meal, we can click on the Skype icon and talk with someone across the world, instantly. The confusing part of this new world is we still have borders that "protect" while the internet continues to tear those walls down.

We have people making stuff in other countries earning those manufacturing dollars. We have universities online available to anyone who can access the internet. We can even conduct transactions of goods and services across the globe with a simple swipe of a credit card.

But we can't allow people to come to this country and be a part of our civilization?

The old arguments about jobs being taken have scant substance. Illegals have little chance to be vocationally mobile because of the fear of deportation, so most of the illegal jobs are reduced to hourly work for cash. They stay off the grid as best as they can because any ping on the radar of Immigration and Naturalization Service can send them packing.

So think about the jobs you can do for cash: day labor, restaurant backroom help, farmers, subcontractor builders. Most of these jobs take a tremendous amount of manual labor. Now, I work with high school and college graduates, and I can write with confidence to say there is no high school senior looking to fill these jobs. The truth of the matter lies in the heart of all of us.

Can we engage in a real discussion with the principles of Jesus at the forefront of our conversation?

Conclusion

Who is going to harm you if you are eager to do good? But
even if you should suffer for what is right, you are blessed.
"Do not fear their threats; do not be frightened."

1 Peter 3.13–14

Fear is the most underestimated of all our emotions.

We fear rejection.

We fear failure.

We fear not being good enough.

We fear not performing spiritually and the accompanying
guilt.

We fear change.

We fear the "other."

All these feelings create a whole paradigm through which
we see the world. I realize the fears raised in this book could
be the source for much controversy. I understand there are
conflicting views on faith, politics, economy, and war, but we
need to at least have these conversations so we can overcome
the feelings of fear that control our lives.

It seems trite to say, "For God did not give us this spirit of fear" and then go right on listening to the latest media talking head who continues to promote that fear, or give in to the fears that are driving our lives, without a level-headed conversation.

I would propose that if you are serious about getting rid of the fear in your life, you take a few beginning steps to understanding how fear is controlling your life.

Free from Fear

What would it look like if we adopted a way of living free from fear?

It begins with an understanding of who God is and what His relationship with humanity is. It's hard to be afraid of the world around you when you commune with the God of the universe who created all things and in whom all things hold together.

After all, if God created us and loved us enough to engage in the world with us, sending a sacrifice for us, where do we have room to be afraid?

I understand it's not realistic to just stand before the throne of heaven and say, "Okay, I'm not going to be afraid anymore."

Fear is real. It's a real thing that appears like a shadow on the sidewalk on a sunny afternoon. Sometimes there's just nothing you can do to stop it.

Paul wrote about ways to overcome fear, saying, "We destroy arguments and every lofty opinion raised against the knowledge of God, and take every thought captive to obey Christ" (2 Cor. 10:5 ESV).

Sometimes it's not about forcing ourselves to overcome fear but about actually redirecting every thought we have in obedience to how God has called us to think. Romans 12:2 says, "Do not conform to the pattern of this world, but be transformed by the renewing of your mind."

It's this "renewal of the mind" that acts as an exercise to train our minds to stop the fear that overcomes us.

Free from the Fear of Others

What if we saw the whole of humanity—no matter what they look like, believe like, act like, or worship like—as God sees them?

Much of our fear today comes from ignorance.

It's not that we're stupid; we just don't take the time to know people in their culture, in their environment, and in their world. We're so busy thinking about how to make the world a better place we forget that maybe people like living in their world just the way they are.

We don't take the time to really get to know someone else and be known by them. We're concerned with our world, focused on our worldview, and have little time to afford to another.

Conquering our fear of the "other" starts with understanding the world through their eyes. Trying to understand the way someone else grew up helps identify the worldview baggage they deal with. The pain of loss, the pain of rejection, the pain of not measuring up; these all are ways we can begin communicating with people we're scared of.

The old cliché about walking a mile in someone else's shoes is true. Before we pass judgment on someone else, we need to know where they've come from. And understanding leads to *freedom*.

Free from Others' Fear

What if our mantra for living in the world was to help people be free from the fear that drives them to act in ways we don't agree with?

The art of healthy dialogue has been lost in our modern world. We tend to watch experts on the news who yell at each other for two and a half minutes, and the winner of the debate is the one who yelled the loudest. This practice has done nothing to help us reach out and discuss things in a civilized disagreement. It promotes anger, yelling, and extremism.

We can see it in politics, economy, and global events. It seems like the more extreme you are, the more you win the adoration of the people who follow you.

But what would happen if we started to approach relationships with the same care and concern God has for "others"? Surely we don't think God is only on our side! The Bible says God causes the rain to fall on both the righteous and the unrighteous (see Matt. 5:45).

God loves people. He's not afraid of knowing them. In fact, He wants to engage in the lives of humanity.

The fear of the other may dissipate when we take a godly approach to loving humanity.

Free from Labels

What if we became ambassadors who are known for peace and unconditional love rather than those who feel the need to defend our own standard of right?

As we approach living in a post-Christian world, we have to recognize that many people are outright afraid of Christians.

They think we're only in our faith to convince or contrive others to do the same. Churches have been known more for their attention to economic issues rather than their attention to taking care of the communities around them.

I have a longstanding discussion with a Lebanese friend who says, "We used to love American Christians because they brought schools, hospitals, and businesses. Today, all we know of Christian America is war and violence." I believe that's an extreme statement, but it might also be an indicator of how we are living out our faith, even back in our homes.

Do people know you for what you're *for*, or simply what you're *against*? Are people attracted to the hope you are living, or do they run the other way because of the reputation Christians have of being hypocritical and judgmental?

The bonds of trust can turn these feelings of fear from anxiousness to friendship, if we only hold true to the faith principles we say we belong to.

I believe it can happen. I've seen it happen. I've watched thousands of teenagers and university students become willing to look each other in the eye and develop a fertile sense of knowing each other deeply.

I've been a part of helping people look their deepest fears right in the face and come to the realization that "God so loved the *world*." I've watched as they were willing to begin working on the fears and prejudices that lace our hearts with shadows of doubt and discomfort.

We can do this, but it requires us to stop listening to the drumbeat of fear driving us to action and to spend the same energy learning how to care for each other.

Having no fear in love isn't about being silly and ignorant. It's about being confident enough in our own relationship with God that nothing can stand in our way of loving another human being.

God did not give us this spirit of fear. In order to align our theological living with our practical everyday relationships, we all need to take a long, hard look and identify our most fearful areas, and begin to face those fears with a deep well of compassion for others.

About the Author

Andy Braner is a minister and the former president of Kanakuk Colorado Kamp in Bayfield, Colorado. His mission is to create a place where teenagers can explore their faith and understand the Christian worldview and to provide opportunities for teenagers to engage in God's work around the world.

Andy recently started a nonprofit camping ministry called Ahava Ministries. The first location is KIVU (www.campkivu .com), where a team of college students provides Christian worldview training to teenagers for fourteen-day terms each summer. Andy teaches Christian worldview classes to approximately a thousand teenagers and three hundred college-age counselors each summer. His desire is to teach young people what it means to be "Realife/Realfaith" followers of Jesus.

KIVU has started a gap-year program for high school students to participate in during the year between graduation and their freshman year of college. This program is proving to be a wonderful opportunity for students to explore issues such as poverty and God's view of the poor, international business, and global relationships with different countries. You can learn more about the gap year at www.kivugapyear.com.

In an average year, Andy speaks to more than eighty thousand high school and college students in both public and private schools. He teaches on a wide variety of topics, including teen sexuality, how Christians engage in culture, Christians in arts and entertainment, world religions, and the biggest plague in humanity today: loneliness. He frequently speaks at youth conferences, churches, schools, and universities.

Andy lives with his wife and five children in Durango, Colorado, where they continue to seek God's will for their family.

FOLLOW

Andy Braner

ON

His Journey

VISIT ANDYBRANER.COM

 @BRANER

FACEBOOK.COM/BRANER

• • •

Andy is a popular blogger and continues to hold the #10 spot on Facebook's Network Blogs with over 70K subscribers. His blog pushes the envelope of what popular Christian culture thinks and its view on the world in a way that brings a wholeness and deeper understanding on attitudes, beliefs, and the world as a whole.

CAMP KIVU

Not your normal summer camp!
High-energy adventures
while learning to love God + others

We host students from twenty-two different countries
to explore adventures in Colorado while serving up
a conversation of faith, culture, and friendship.

campkivu.com 970-884-1100

KIVU GAP YEAR

Develop a life thesis and get college credit!
Vocational discovery in a global community

Experience the cultures and contexts of peoples
from around the world with over nine hundred hours of
internship experience in more than five countries.

Kivugapyear.com 970-884-1100